THE ANGEL IN THE HOUSE

By
Coventry Patmore

INTRODUCTION.

There could be but one answer to the suggestion of Mr. Coventry Patmore that his "Angel in the House" might usefully have a place in this "National Library." The suggestion was made with the belief that wide and cheap diffusion would not take from the value of a copyright library edition, while the best use of writing is fulfilled by the spreading of verse dedicated to the sacred love of home. The two parts of the Poem appeared in 1854 and 1856, were afterwards elaborately revised, and have since obtained a permanent place among the Home Books of the English People. Our readers will join, surely, in thanks to the author for the present he has made us.

H. M.

THE ANGEL IN THE HOUSE

BOOK I.

THE PROLOGUE.

1

'Mine is no horse with wings, to gain
The region of the spheral chime;
He does but drag a rumbling wain,
Cheer'd by the coupled bells of rhyme;
And if at Fame's bewitching note
My homely Pegasus pricks an ear,
The world's cart-collar hugs his throat,
And he's too wise to prance or rear.'

2

Thus ever answer'd Vaughan his Wife,
Who, more than he, desired his fame;
But, in his heart, his thoughts were rife
How for her sake to earn a name.
With bays poetic three times crown'd,
And other college honours won,
He, if he chose, might be renown'd,
He had but little doubt, she none;
And in a loftier phrase he talk'd
With her, upon their Wedding-Day,

3

(The eighth), while through the fields they walk'd,
Their children shouting by the way.
'Not careless of the gift of song,
Nor out of love with noble fame,
I, meditating much and long
What I should sing, how win a name,
Considering well what theme unsung,
What reason worth the cost of rhyme,
Remains to loose the poet's tongue
In these last days, the dregs of time,
Learn that to me, though born so late,
There does, beyond desert, befall
(May my great fortune make me great!)
The first of themes, sung last of all.
In green and undiscover'd ground,
Yet near where many others sing,
I have the very well-head found
Whence gushes the Pierian Spring.'

4

Then she: 'What is it, Dear? The Life
Of Arthur, or Jerusalem's Fall?'
'Neither: your gentle self, my Wife,
And love, that grows from one to all.
And if I faithfully proclaim
Of these the exceeding worthiness,
Surely the sweetest wreath of Fame
Shall, to your hope, my brows caress;
And if, by virtue of my choice
Of this, the most heart-touching theme
That ever tuned a poet's voice,
I live, as I am bold to dream,
To be delight to many days,
And into silence only cease
When those are still, who shared their bays
With Laura and with Beatrice,
Imagine, Love, how learned men
Will deep-conceiv'd devices find,
Beyond my purpose and my ken,
An ancient bard of simple mind.
You, Sweet, his Mistress, Wife, and Muse,
Were you for mortal woman meant?
Your praises give a hundred clues
To mythological intent!
And, severing thus the truth from trope,
In you the Commentators see

4

Outlines occult of abstract scope,
A future for philosophy!
Your arm's on mine! these are the meads
In which we pass our living days;
There Avon runs, now hid with reeds,
Now brightly brimming pebbly bays;
Those are our children's songs that come
With bells and bleatings of the sheep;
And there, in yonder English home,
We thrive on mortal food and sleep!'
She laugh'd. How proud she always was
To feel how proud he was of her!
But he had grown distraught, because
The Muse's mood began to stir.

5

His purpose with performance crown'd,
He to his well-pleased Wife rehears'd,
When next their Wedding-Day came round,
His leisure's labour, 'Book the First.'

CANTO I—THE CATHEDRAL CLOSE.

PRELUDES.

I.—The Impossibility.

Lo, love's obey'd by all. 'Tis right
That all should know what they obey,
Lest erring conscience damp delight,
And folly laugh our joys away.
Thou Primal Love, who grantest wings
And voices to the woodland birds,
Grant me the power of saying things
Too simple and too sweet for words!

II.—Love's Really.

I walk, I trust, with open eyes;
I've travell'd half my worldly course;
And in the way behind me lies
Much vanity and some remorse;
I've lived to feel how pride may part
Spirits, tho' match'd like hand and glove;
I've blush'd for love's abode, the heart;
But have not disbelieved in love;
Nor unto love, sole mortal thing

Of worth immortal, done the wrong
To count it, with the rest that sing,
Unworthy of a serious song;
And love is my reward; for now,
When most of dead'ning time complain,
The myrtle blooms upon my brow,
Its odour quickens all my brain.

III.—The Poet's Confidence.

The richest realm of all the earth
Is counted still a heathen land:
Lo, I, like Joshua, now go forth
To give it into Israel's hand.
I will not hearken blame or praise;
For so should I dishonour do
To that sweet Power by which these Lays
Alone are lovely, good, and true;
Nor credence to the world's cries give,
Which ever preach and still prevent
Pure passion's high prerogative
To make, not follow, precedent.
From love's abysmal ether rare
If I to men have here made known
New truths, they, like new stars, were there
Before, though not yet written down.
Moving but as the feelings move,
I run, or loiter with delight,
Or pause to mark where gentle Love
Persuades the soul from height to height.
Yet, know ye, though my words are gay
As David's dance, which Michal scorn'd.
If kindly you receive the Lay,
You shall be sweetly help'd and warn'd.

THE CATHEDRAL CLOSE.

1.

Once more I came to Sarum Close,
With joy half memory, half desire,
And breathed the sunny wind that rose
And blew the shadows o'er the Spire,
And toss'd the lilac's scented plumes,
And sway'd the chestnut's thousand cones,
And fill'd my nostrils with perfumes,
And shaped the clouds in waifs and zones,
And wafted down the serious strain

Of Sarum bells, when, true to time,
I reach'd the Dean's, with heart and brain
That trembled to the trembling chime.

2

'Twas half my home, six years ago.
The six years had not alter'd it:
Red-brick and ashlar, long and low,
With dormers and with oriels lit.
Geranium, lychnis, rose array'd
The windows, all wide open thrown;
And some one in the Study play'd
The Wedding-March of Mendelssohn.
And there it was I last took leave:
'Twas Christmas: I remember'd now
The cruel girls, who feign'd to grieve,
Took down the evergreens; and how
The holly into blazes woke
The fire, lighting the large, low room,
A dim, rich lustre of old oak
And crimson velvet's glowing gloom.
No change had touch'd Dean Churchill: kind,
By widowhood more than winters bent,
And settled in a cheerful mind,
As still forecasting heaven's content.
Well might his thoughts be fix'd on high,
Now she was there! Within her face
Humility and dignity
Were met in a most sweet embrace.
She seem'd expressly sent below
To teach our erring minds to see
The rhythmic change of time's swift flow
As part of still eternity.
Her life, all honour, observed, with awe
Which cross experience could not mar,
The fiction of the Christian law
That all men honourable are;
And so her smile at once conferr'd
High flattery and benign reproof;
And I, a rude boy, strangely stirr'd,
Grew courtly in my own behoof.
The years, so far from doing her wrong,
Anointed her with gracious balm,
And made her brows more and more young
With wreaths of amaranth and palm.

4

Was this her eldest, Honor; prude,
Who would not let me pull the swing;
Who, kiss'd at Christmas, call'd me rude,
And, sobbing low, refused to sing?
How changed! In shape no slender Grace,
But Venus; milder than the dove;
Her mother's air; her Norman face;
Her large sweet eyes, clear lakes of love.
Mary I knew. In former time
Ailing and pale, she thought that bliss
Was only for a better clime,
And, heavenly overmuch, scorn'd this.
I, rash with theories of the right,
Which stretch'd the tether of my Creed,
But did not break it, held delight
Half discipline. We disagreed.
She told the Dean I wanted grace.
Now she was kindest of the three,
And soft wild roses deck'd her face.
And, what, was this my Mildred, she
To herself and all a sweet surprise?
My Pet, who romp'd and roll'd a hoop?
I wonder'd where those daisy eyes
Had found their touching curve and droop.

5

Unmannerly times! But now we sat
Stranger than strangers; till I caught
And answer'd Mildred's smile; and that
Spread to the rest, and freedom brought.
The Dean talk'd little, looking on,
Of three such daughters justly vain.
What letters they had had from Bonn,
Said Mildred, and what plums from Spain!
By Honor I was kindly task'd
To excuse my never coming down
From Cambridge; Mary smiled and ask'd
Were Kant and Goethe yet outgrown?
And, pleased, we talk'd the old days o'er;
And, parting, I for pleasure sigh'd.
To be there as a friend, (since more),
Seem'd then, seems still, excuse for pride;
For something that abode endued
With temple-like repose, an air
Of life's kind purposes pursued
With order'd freedom sweet and fair.

A tent pitch'd in a world not right
It seem'd, whose inmates, every one,
On tranquil faces bore the light
Of duties beautifully done,
And humbly, though they had few peers,
Kept their own laws, which seem'd to be
The fair sum of six thousand years'
Traditions of civility.

CANTO II—MARY AND MILDRED

PRELUDES.

I.—The Paragon.

When I behold the skies aloft
Passing the pageantry of dreams,
The cloud whose bosom, cygnet-soft,
A couch for nuptial Juno seems,
The ocean broad, the mountains bright,
The shadowy vales with feeding herds,
I from my lyre the music smite,
Nor want for justly matching words.
All forces of the sea and air,
All interests of hill and plain,
I so can sing, in seasons fair,
That who hath felt may feel again.
Elated oft by such free songs,
I think with utterance free to raise
That hymn for which the whole world longs,
A worthy hymn in woman's praise;
A hymn bright-noted like a bird's,
Arousing these song-sleepy times
With rhapsodies of perfect words,
Ruled by returning kiss of rhymes.
But when I look on her and hope
To tell with joy what I admire,
My thoughts lie cramp'd in narrow scope,
Or in the feeble birth expire;
No mystery of well-woven speech,
No simplest phrase of tenderest fall,
No liken'd excellence can reach
Her, thee most excellent of all,
The best half of creation's best,
Its heart to feel, its eye to see,
The crown and complex of the rest,

9

Its aim and its epitome.
Nay, might I utter my conceit,
'Twere after all a vulgar song,
For she's so simply, subtly sweet,
My deepest rapture does her wrong.
Yet is it now my chosen task
To sing her worth as Maid and Wife;
Nor happier post than this I ask,
To live her laureate all my life.
On wings of love uplifted free,
And by her gentleness made great,
I'll teach how noble man should be
To match with such a lovely mate;
And then in her may move the more
The woman's wish to be desired,
(By praise increased), till both shall soar,
With blissful emulations fired.
And, as geranium, pink, or rose
Is thrice itself through power of art,
So may my happy skill disclose
New fairness even in her fair heart;
Until that churl shall nowhere be
Who bends not, awed, before the throne
Of her affecting majesty,
So meek, so far unlike our own;
Until (for who may hope too much
From her who wields the powers of love?)
Our lifted lives at last shall touch
That happy goal to which they move;
Until we find, as darkness rolls
Away, and evil mists dissolve,
That nuptial contrasts are the poles
On which the heavenly spheres revolve.

II.—Love at Large.

Whene'er I come where ladies are,
How sad soever I was before,
Though like a ship frost-bound and far
Withheld in ice from the ocean's roar,
Third-winter'd in that dreadful dock,
With stiffen'd cordage, sails decay'd,
And crew that care for calm and shock
Alike, too dull to be dismay'd,
Yet, if I come where ladies are,
How sad soever I was before,
Then is my sadness banish'd far,

And I am like that ship no more;
Or like that ship if the ice-field splits,
Burst by the sudden polar Spring,
And all thank God with their warming wits,
And kiss each other and dance and sing,
And hoist fresh sails, that make the breeze
Blow them along the liquid sea,
Out of the North, where life did freeze,
Into the haven where they would be.

III.—Love and Duty.

Anne lived so truly from above,
She was so gentle and so good,
That duty bade me fall in love,
And 'but for that,' thought I, 'I should!'
I worshipp'd Kate with all my will,
In idle moods you seem to see
A noble spirit in a hill,
A human touch about a tree.

IV.—A Distinction.

The lack of lovely pride, in her
Who strives to please, my pleasure numbs,
And still the maid I most prefer
Whose care to please with pleasing comes.

MARY AND MILDRED.

1

One morning, after Church, I walk'd
Alone with Mary on the lawn,
And felt myself, howe'er we talk'd,
To grave themes delicately drawn.
When she, delighted, found I knew
More of her peace than she supposed,
Our confidences heavenwards grew,
Like fox-glove buds, in pairs disclosed.
Our former faults did we confess,
Our ancient feud was more than heal'd,
And, with the woman's eagerness
For amity full-sign'd and seal'd,
She, offering up for sacrifice
Her heart's reserve, brought out to show
Some verses, made when she was ice
To all but Heaven, six years ago;
Since happier grown! I took and read

11

The neat-writ lines. She, void of guile,
Too late repenting, blush'd, and said,
I must not think about the style.

2

'Day after day, until to-day,
Imaged the others gone before,
The same dull task, the weary way,
The weakness pardon'd o'er and o'er,

'The thwarted thirst, too faintly felt,
For joy's well-nigh forgotten life,
The restless heart, which, when I knelt,
Made of my worship barren strife.

'Ah, whence to-day's so sweet release,
This clearance light of all my care,
This conscience free, this fertile peace,
These softly folded wings of prayer,

'This calm and more than conquering love,
With which nought evil dares to cope,
This joy that lifts no glance above,
For faith too sure, too sweet for hope?

'O, happy time, too happy change,
It will not live, though fondly nurst!
Full soon the sun will seem as strange
As now the cloud which seems dispersed.'

3

She from a rose-tree shook the blight;
And well she knew that I knew well
Her grace with silence to requite;
And, answering now the luncheon bell,
I laugh'd at Mildred's laugh, which made
All melancholy wrong, its mood
Such sweet self-confidence display'd,
So glad a sense of present good.

4

I laugh'd and sigh'd: for I confess
I never went to Ball, or Fete,
Or Show, but in pursuit express
Of my predestinated mate;
And thus to me, who had in sight
The happy chance upon the cards,
Each beauty blossom'd in the light
Of tender personal regards;

And, in the records of my breast,
Red-letter'd, eminently fair,
Stood sixteen, who, beyond the rest,
By turns till then had been my care:
At Berlin three, one at St. Cloud,
At Chatteris, near Cambridge, one,
At Ely four, in London two,
Two at Bowness, in Paris none,
And, last and best, in Sarum three;
But dearest of the whole fair troop,
In judgment of the moment, she
Whose daisy eyes had learn'd to droop.
Her very faults my fancy fired;
My loving will, so thwarted, grew;
And, bent on worship, I admired
Whate'er she was, with partial view.
And yet when, as to-day, her smile
Was prettiest, I could not but note
Honoria, less admired the while,
Was lovelier, though from love remote.

CANTO III.—Honoria

PRELUDES.

I.—The Lover.

He meets, by heavenly chance express,
The destined maid; seine hidden hand
Unveils to him that loveliness
Which others cannot understand.
His merits in her presence grow,
To match the promise in her eyes,
And round her happy footsteps blow
The authentic airs of Paradise.
For joy of her he cannot sleep;
Her beauty haunts him all the night;
It melts his heart, it makes him weep
For wonder, worship, and delight.
O, paradox of love, he longs,
Most humble when he most aspires,
To suffer scorn and cruel wrongs
From her he honours and desires.
Her graces make him rich, and ask
No guerdon; this imperial style
Affronts him; he disdains to bask,
The pensioner of her priceless smile.

13

He prays for some hard thing to do,
Some work of fame and labour immense,
To stretch the languid bulk and thew
Of love's fresh-born magnipotence.
No smallest boon were bought too dear,
Though barter'd for his love-sick life;
Yet trusts he, with undaunted cheer,
To vanquish heaven, and call her Wife
He notes how queens of sweetness still
Neglect their crowns, and stoop to mate;
How, self-consign'd with lavish will,
They ask but love proportionate;
How swift pursuit by small degrees,
Love's tactic, works like miracle;
How valour, clothed in courtesies,
Brings down the haughtiest citadel;
And therefore, though he merits not
To kiss the braid upon her skirt,
His hope, discouraged ne'er a jot,
Out-soars all possible desert.

II.—Love a Virtue.

Strong passions mean weak will, and he
Who truly knows the strength and bliss
Which are in love, will own with me
No passion but a virtue 'tis.
Few hear my word; it soars above
The subtlest senses of the swarm
Of wretched things which know not love,
Their Psyche still a wingless worm.
Ice-cold seems heaven's noble glow
To spirits whose vital heat is hell;
And to corrupt hearts even so
The songs I sing, the tale I tell.
These cannot see the robes of white
In which I sing of love. Alack,
But darkness shows in heavenly light,
Though whiteness, in the dark, is black!

III.—The Attainment.

You love? That's high as you shall go;
For 'tis as true as Gospel text,
Not noble then is never so,
Either in this world or the next.

HONORIA.

1

Grown weary with a week's exile
From those fair friends, I rode to see
The church-restorings; lounged awhile,
And met the Dean; was ask'd to tea,
And found their cousin, Frederick Graham
At Honor's side. Was I concern'd,
If, when she sang, his colour came,
That mine, as with a buffet, burn'd?
A man to please a girl! thought I,
Retorting his forced smiles, the shrouds
Of wrath, so hid as she was by,
Sweet moon between her lighted clouds!

2

Whether this Cousin was the cause
I know not, but I seem'd to see,
The first time then, how fair she was,
How much the fairest of the three.
Each stopp'd to let the other go;
But, time-bound, he arose the first.
Stay'd he in Sarum long? If so
I hoped to see him at the Hurst.
No: he had call'd here, on his way
To Portsmouth, where the Arrogant,
His ship, was; he should leave next day,
For two years' cruise in the Levant.

3

Had love in her yet struck its germs?
I watch'd. Her farewell show'd me plain
She loved, on the majestic terms
That she should not be loved again;
And so her cousin, parting, felt.
Hope in his voice and eye was dead.
Compassion did my malice melt;
Then went I home to a restless bed.
I, who admired her too, could see
His infinite remorse at this
Great mystery, that she should be
So beautiful, yet not be his,
And, pitying, long'd to plead his part;
But scarce could tell, so strange my whim,
Whether the weight upon my heart
Was sorrow for myself or him.

4

She was all mildness; yet 'twas writ
In all her grace, most legibly,
'He that's for heaven itself unfit,
Let him not hope to merit me.'
And such a challenge, quite apart
From thoughts of love, humbled, and thus
To sweet repentance moved my heart,
And made me more magnanimous,
And led me to review my life,
Inquiring where in aught the least,
If question were of her for wife,
Ill might be mended, hope increas'd.
Not that I soar'd so far above
Myself, as this great hope to dare;
And yet I well foresaw that love
Might hope where reason must despair;
And, half-resenting the sweet pride
Which would not ask me to admire,
'Oh,' to my secret heart I sigh'd,
'That I were worthy to desire!'

5

As drowsiness my brain reliev'd,
A shrill defiance of all to arms,
Shriek'd by the stable-cock, receiv'd
An angry answer from three farms.
And, then, I dream'd that I, her knight,
A clarion's haughty pathos heard,
And rode securely to the fight,
Cased in the scarf she had conferr'd;
And there, the bristling lists behind,
Saw many, and vanquish'd all I saw
Of her unnumber'd cousin-kind,
In Navy, Army, Church, and Law;
Smitten, the warriors somehow turn'd
To Sarum choristers, whose song,
Mix'd with celestial sorrow, yearn'd
With joy no memory can prolong;
And phantasms as absurd and sweet
Merged each in each in endless chace,
And everywhere I seem'd to meet
The haunting fairness of her face.

CANTO IV.—THE MORNING CALL

PRELUDES.

I.—The Rose of the World.

Lo, when the Lord made North and South
And sun and moon ordained, He,
Forthbringing each by word of mouth
In order of its dignity,
Did man from the crude clay express
By sequence, and, all else decreed,
He form'd the woman; nor might less
Than Sabbath such a work succeed.
And still with favour singled out,
Marr'd less than man by mortal fall,
Her disposition is devout,
Her countenance angelical;
The best things that the best believe
Are in her face so kindly writ
The faithless, seeing her, conceive
Not only heaven, but hope of it;
No idle thought her instinct shrouds,
But fancy chequers settled sense,
Like alteration of the clouds
On noonday's azure permanence;
Pure dignity, composure, ease
Declare affections nobly fix'd,
And impulse sprung from due degrees
Of sense and spirit sweetly mix'd.
Her modesty, her chiefest grace,
The cestus clasping Venus' side,
How potent to deject the face
Of him who would affront its pride!
Wrong dares not in her presence speak,
Nor spotted thought its taint disclose
Under the protest of a cheek
Outbragging Nature's boast the rose.
In mind and manners how discreet;
How artless in her very art;
How candid in discourse; how sweet
The concord of her lips and heart;
How simple and how circumspect;
How subtle and how fancy-free;
Though sacred to her love, how deck'd
With unexclusive courtesy;

How quick in talk to see from far
The way to vanquish or evade;
How able her persuasions are
To prove, her reasons to persuade;
How (not to call true instinct's bent
And woman's very nature, harm),
How amiable and innocent
Her pleasure in her power to charm;
How humbly careful to attract,
Though crown'd with all the soul desires,
Connubial aptitude exact,
Diversity that never tires.

II.—The Tribute.

Boon Nature to the woman bows;
She walks in earth's whole glory clad,
And, chiefest far herself of shows,
All others help her, and are glad:
No splendour 'neath the sky's proud dome
But serves for her familiar wear;
The far-fetch'd diamond finds its home
Flashing and smouldering in her hair;
For her the seas their pearls reveal;
Art and strange lands her pomp supply
With purple, chrome, and cochineal,
Ochre, and lapis lazuli;
The worm its golden woof presents;
Whatever runs, flies, dives, or delves,
All doff for her their ornaments,
Which suit her better than themselves;
And all, by this their power to give,
Proving her right to take, proclaim
Her beauty's clear prerogative
To profit so by Eden's blame.

III.—Compensation.

That nothing here may want its praise,
Know, she who in her dress reveals
A fine and modest taste, displays
More loveliness than she conceals.

THE MORNING CALL.

1

'By meekness charm'd, or proud to allow
A queenly claim to live admired,

18

Full many a lady has ere now
My apprehensive fancy fired,
And woven many a transient chain;
But never lady like to this,
Who holds me as the weather-vane
Is held by yonder clematis.
She seems the life of nature's powers;
Her beauty is the genial thought
Which makes the sunshine bright; the flowers,
But for their hint of her, were nought.'

2

A voice, the sweeter for the grace
Of suddenness, while thus I dream'd,
'Good morning!' said or sang. Her face
The mirror of the morning seem'd.
Her sisters in the garden walk'd,
And would I come? Across the Hall
She led me; and we laugh'd and talk'd,
And praised the Flower-show and the Ball;
And Mildred's pinks had gain'd the Prize;
And, stepping like the light-foot fawn,
She brought me 'Wiltshire Butterflies,'
The Prize-book; then we paced the lawn,
Close-cut, and with geranium-plots,
A rival glow of green and red;
Than counted sixty apricots
On one small tree; the gold-fish fed;
And watch'd where, black with scarlet tans,
Proud Psyche stood and flash'd like flame,
Showing and shutting splendid fans;
And in the prize we found its name.

3

The sweet hour lapsed, and left my breast
A load of joy and tender care;
And this delight, which life oppress'd,
To fix'd aims grew, that ask'd for pray'r.
I rode home slowly; whip-in-hand
And soil'd bank-notes all ready, stood
The Farmer who farm'd all my land,
Except the little Park and Wood;
And with the accustom'd compliment
Of talk, and beef, and frothing beer,
I, my own steward, took my rent,
Three hundred pounds for half the year;

19

Our witnesses the Cook and Groom,
We sign'd the lease for seven years more,
And bade Good-day; then to my room
I went, and closed and lock'd the door,
And cast myself down on my bed,
And there, with many a blissful tear,
I vow'd to love and pray'd to wed
The maiden who had grown so dear;
Thank'd God who had set her in my path;
And promised, as I hoped to win,
That I would never dim my faith
By the least selfishness or sin;
Whatever in her sight I'd seem
I'd truly be; I'd never blend
With my delight in her a dream
'Twould change her cheek to comprehend;
And, if she wish'd it, I'd prefer
Another's to my own success;
And always seek the best for her
With unofficious tenderness.

4

Rising, I breathed a brighter clime,
And found myself all self above,
And, with a charity sublime,
Contemn'd not those who did not love:
And I could not but feel that then
I shone with something of her grace,
And went forth to my fellow men
My commendation in my face.

CANTO V.—THE VIOLETS

PRELUDES.

I.—The Comparison.

Where she succeeds with cloudless brow,
In common and in holy course,
He fails, in spite of prayer and vow
And agonies of faith and force;
Or, if his suit with Heaven prevails
To righteous life, his virtuous deeds
Lack beauty, virtue's badge; she fails
More graciously than he succeeds.
Her spirit, compact of gentleness,

If Heaven postpones or grants her pray'r,
Conceives no pride in its success,
And in its failure no despair;
But his, enamour'd of its hurt,
Baffled, blasphemes, or, not denied,
Crows from the dunghill of desert,
And wags its ugly wings for pride.
He's never young nor ripe; she grows
More infantine, auroral, mild,
And still the more she lives and knows
The lovelier she's express'd a child.
Say that she wants the will of man
To conquer fame, not check'd by cross,
Nor moved when others bless or ban;
She wants but what to have were loss.
Or say she wants the patient brain
To track shy truth; her facile wit
At that which he hunts down with pain
Flies straight, and does exactly hit.
Were she but half of what she is,
He twice himself, mere love alone,
Her special crown, as truth is his,
Gives title to the worthier throne;
For love is substance, truth the form;
Truth without love were less than nought;
But blindest love is sweet and warm,
And full of truth not shaped by thought,
And therefore in herself she stands
Adorn'd with undeficient grace,
Her happy virtues taking hands,
Each smiling in another's face.
So, dancing round the Tree of Life,
They make an Eden in her breast,
While his, disjointed and at strife,
Proud-thoughted, do not bring him rest.

II.—Love in Tears.

If fate Love's dear ambition mar,
And load his breast with hopeless pain,
And seem to blot out sun and star,
Love, won or lost, is countless gain;
His sorrow boasts a secret bliss
Which sorrow of itself beguiles,
And Love in tears too noble is
For pity, save of Love in smiles.
But, looking backward through his tears,

With vision of maturer scope,
How often one dead joy appears
The platform of some better hope!
And, let us own, the sharpest smart
Which human patience may endure
Pays light for that which leaves the heart
More generous, dignified, and pure.

III.—PROSPECTIVE FAITH.

They safely walk in darkest ways
Whose youth is lighted from above,
Where, through the senses' silvery haze,
Dawns the veil'd moon of nuptial love.
Who is the happy husband? He
Who, scanning his unwedded life,
Thanks Heaven, with a conscience free,
'Twas faithful to his future wife.

IV.—VENUS VICTRIX.

Fatal in force, yet gentle in will,
Defeats, from her, are tender pacts,
For, like the kindly lodestone, still
She's drawn herself by what she attracts.

THE VIOLETS.

1

I went not to the Dean's unbid:
I would not have my mystery,
From her so delicately hid,
The guess of gossips at their tea.
A long, long week, and not once there,
Had made my spirit sick and faint,
And lack-love, foul as love is fair,
Perverted all things to complaint.
How vain the world had grown to be!
How mean all people and their ways,
How ignorant their sympathy,
And how impertinent their praise;
What they for virtuousness esteem'd,
How far removed from heavenly right;
What pettiness their trouble seem'd,
How undelightful their delight;
To my necessity how strange
The sunshine and the song of birds;

How dull the clouds' continual change,
How foolishly content the herds;
How unaccountable the law
Which bade me sit in blindness here,
While she, the sun by which I saw,
Shed splendour in an idle sphere!
And then I kiss'd her stolen glove,
And sigh'd to reckon and define
The modes of martyrdom in love,
And how far each one might be mine.
I thought how love, whose vast estate
Is earth and air and sun and sea,
Encounters oft the beggar's fate,
Despised on score of poverty;
How Heaven, inscrutable in this,
Lets the gross general make or mar
The destiny of love, which is
So tender and particular;
How nature, as unnatural
And contradicting nature's source,
Which is but love, seems most of all
Well-pleased to harry true love's course;
How, many times, it comes to pass
That trifling shades of temperament,
Affecting only one, alas,
Not love, but love's success prevent;
How manners often falsely paint
The man; how passionate respect,
Hid by itself, may bear the taint
Of coldness and a dull neglect;
And how a little outward dust
Can a clear merit quite o'ercloud,
And make her fatally unjust,
And him desire a darker shroud;
How senseless opportunity
Gives baser men the better chance;
How powers, adverse else, agree
To cheat her in her ignorance;
How Heaven its very self conspires
With man and nature against love,
As pleased to couple cross desires,
And cross where they themselves approve.
Wretched were life, if the end were now!
But this gives tears to dry despair,
Faith shall be blest, we know not how,
And love fulfill'd, we know not where.

2

While thus I grieved, and kiss'd her glove,
My man brought in her note to say,
Papa had hid her send his love,
And would I dine with them next day?
They had learn'd and practised Purcell's glee,
To sing it by to-morrow night.
The Postscript was: Her sisters and she
Inclosed some violets, blue and white;
She and her sisters found them where
I wager'd once no violets grew;
So they had won the gloves. And there
The violets lay, two white, one blue.

CANTO VI.—THE DEAN

PRELUDES.

I.—PERFECT LOVE RARE.

Most rare is still most noble found,
Most noble still most incomplete;
Sad law, which leaves King Love uncrown'd
In this obscure, terrestrial seat!
With bale more sweet than others' bliss,
And bliss more wise than others' bale,
The secrets of the world are his.
And freedom without let or pale.
O, zealous good, O, virtuous glee,
Religious, and without alloy,
O, privilege high, which none but he
Who highly merits can enjoy;
O, Love, who art that fabled sun
Which all the world with bounty loads,
Without respect of realms, save one,
And gilds with double lustre Rhodes;
A day of whose delicious life,
Though full of terrors, full of tears,
Is better than of other life
A hundred thousand million years;
Thy heavenly splendour magnifies
The least commixture of earth's mould,
Cheapens thyself in thine own eyes,
And makes the foolish mocker bold.

II.—LOVE JUSTIFIED.

What if my pole-star of respect
Be dim to others? Shall their 'Nay,'
Presumably their own defect,
Invalidate my heart's strong 'Yea'?
And can they rightly me condemn,
If I, with partial love, prefer?
I am not more unjust to them,
But only not unjust to her.
Leave us alone! After awhile,
This pool of private charity
Shall make its continent an isle,
And roll, a world-embracing sea;
This foolish zeal of lip for lip,
This fond, self-sanction'd, wilful zest,
Is that elect relationship
Which forms and sanctions all the rest;
This little germ of nuptial love,
Which springs so simply from the sod,
The root is, as my song shall prove,
Of all our love to man and God.

III.—LOVE SERVICEABLE.

What measure Fate to him shall mete
Is not the noble Lover's care;
He's heart-sick with a longing sweet
To make her happy as she's fair.
Oh, misery, should she him refuse,
And so her dearest good mistake!
His own success he thus pursues
With frantic zeal for her sole sake.
To lose her were his life to blight,
Being loss to hers; to make her his,
Except as helping her delight,
He calls but incidental bliss;
And holding life as so much pelf
To buy her posies, learns this lore:
He does not rightly love himself
Who does not love another more.

IV.—A RIDDLE SOLVED.

Kind souls, you wonder why, love you,
When you, you wonder why, love none.
We love, Fool, for the good we do,
Not that which unto us is done!

25

THE DEAN.

1

The Ladies rose. I held the door,
And sigh'd, as her departing grace
Assured me that she always wore
A heart as happy as her face;
And, jealous of the winds that blew,
I dreaded, o'er the tasteless wine,
What fortune momently might do
To hurt the hope that she'd be mine.

2

Towards my mark the Dean's talk set:
He praised my 'Notes on Abury,'
Read when the Association met
At Sarum; he was pleased to see
I had not stopp'd, as some men had,
At Wrangler and Prize Poet; last,
He hoped the business was not bad
I came about: then the wine pass'd.

3

A full glass prefaced my reply:
I loved his daughter, Honor; I told
My estate and prospects; might I try
To win her? At my words so bold
My sick heart sank. Then he: He gave
His glad consent, if I could get
Her love. A dear, good Girl! she'd have
Only three thousand pounds as yet;
More bye and bye. Yes, his good will
Should go with me; he would not stir;
He and my father in old time still
Wish'd I should one day marry her;
But God so seldom lets us take
Our chosen pathway, when it lies
In steps that either mar or make
Or alter others' destinies,
That, though his blessing and his pray'r
Had help'd, should help, my suit, yet he
Left all to me, his passive share
Consent and opportunity.
My chance, he hoped, was good: I'd won
Some name already; friends and place
Appear'd within my reach, but none

Her mind and manners would not grace.
Girls love to see the men in whom
They invest their vanities admired;
Besides, where goodness is, there room
For good to work will be desired.
'Twas so with one now pass'd away;
And what she was at twenty-two,
Honor was now; and he might say
Mine was a choice I could not rue.

4

He ceased, and gave his hand. He had won
(And all my heart was in my word),
From me the affection of a son,
Whichever fortune Heaven conferr'd!
Well, well, would I take more wine? Then go
To her; she makes tea on the lawn
These fine warm afternoons. And so
We went whither my soul was drawn;
And her light-hearted ignorance
Of interest in our discourse
Fill'd me with love, and seem'd to enhance
Her beauty with pathetic force,
As, through the flowery mazes sweet,
Fronting the wind that flutter'd blythe,
And loved her shape, and kiss'd her feet,
Shown to their insteps proud and lithe,
She approach'd, all mildness and young trust,
And ever her chaste and noble air
Gave to love's feast its choicest gust,
A vague, faint augury of despair.

CANTO VII—AETNA AND THE MOON

PRELUDES.

I.—LOVE'S IMMORTALITY.

How vilely 'twere to misdeserve
The poet's gift of perfect speech,
In song to try, with trembling nerve,
The limit of its utmost reach,
Only to sound the wretched praise
Of what to-morrow shall not be;
So mocking with immortal bays
The cross-bones of mortality!

27

I do not thus. My faith is fast
That all the loveliness I sing
Is made to bear the mortal blast,
And blossom in a better Spring.
Doubts of eternity ne'er cross
The Lover's mind, divinely clear;
FOR EVER is the gain or loss
Which maddens him with hope or fear:
So trifles serve for his relief,
And trifles make him sick and pale;
And yet his pleasure and his grief
Are both on a majestic scale.
The chance, indefinitely small,
Of issue infinitely great,
Eclipses finite interests all,
And has the dignity of fate.

II.—HEAVEN AND EARTH.

How long shall men deny the flower
Because its roots are in the earth,
And crave with tears from God the dower
They have, and have despised as dearth,
And scorn as low their human lot,
With frantic pride, too blind to see
That standing on the head makes not
Either for ease or dignity!
But fools shall feel like fools to find
(Too late inform'd) that angels' mirth
Is one in cause, and mode, and kind
With that which they profaned on earth.

AETNA AND THE MOON.

1

To soothe my heart I, feigning, seized
A pen, and, showering tears, declared
My unfeign'd passion; sadly pleased
Only to dream that so I dared.
Thus was the fervid truth confess'd,
But wild with paradox ran the plea.
As wilfully in hope depress'd,
Yet bold beyond hope's warranty:

2

'O, more than dear, be more than just,

And do not deafly shut the door!
I claim no right to speak; I trust
Mercy, not right; yet who has more?
For, if more love makes not more fit,
Of claimants here none's more nor less,
Since your great worth does not permit
Degrees in our unworthiness.
Yet, if there's aught that can be done
With arduous labour of long years,
By which you'll say that you'll be won,
O tell me, and I'll dry my tears.
Ah, no; if loving cannot move,
How foolishly must labour fail!
The use of deeds is to show love;
If signs suffice let these avail:
Your name pronounced brings to my heart
A feeling like the violet's breath,
Which does so much of heaven impart
It makes me amorous of death;
The winds that in the garden toss
The Guelder-roses give me pain,
Alarm me with the dread of loss,
Exhaust me with the dream of gain;
I'm troubled by the clouds that move;
Tired by the breath which I respire;
And ever, like a torch, my love,
Thus agitated, flames the higher;
All's hard that has not you for goal;
I scarce can move my hand to write,
For love engages all my soul,
And leaves the body void of might;
The wings of will spread idly, as do
The bird's that in a vacuum lies;
My breast, asleep with dreams of you,
Forgets to breathe, and bursts in sighs;
I see no rest this side the grave,
No rest nor hope, from you apart;
Your life is in the rose you gave,
Its perfume suffocates my heart;
There's no refreshment in the breeze;
The heaven o'erwhelms me with its blue;
I faint beside the dancing seas;
Winds, skies, and waves are only you;
The thought or act which not intends
You service seems a sin and shame;
In that one only objoct ends

Conscience, religion, honour, fame.
Ah, could I put off love! Could we
Never have met! What calm, what ease!
Nay, but, alas, this remedy
Were ten times worse than the disease!
For when, indifferent, I pursue
The world's best pleasures for relief,
My heart, still sickening back to you,
Finds none like memory of its grief;
And, though 'twere very hell to hear
You felt such misery as I,
All good, save you, were far less dear!
Than is that ill with which I die
Where'er I go, wandering forlorn,
You are the world's love, life, and glee:
Oh, wretchedness not to be borne
If she that's Love should not love me!'

3

I could not write another word,
Through pity for my own distress;
And forth I went, untimely stirr'd
To make my misery more or less.
I went, beneath the heated noon
To where, in her simplicity,
She sate at work; and, as the Moon
On AEtna smiles, she smiled on me.
But, now and then, in cheek and eyes,
I saw, or fancied, such a glow
As when, in summer-evening skies,
Some say, 'It lightens,' some say, 'No.'
'Honoria,' I began—No more.
The Dean, by ill or happy hap,
Came home; and Wolf burst in before,
And put his nose upon her lap.

CANTO VIII.—SARUM PLAIN

PRELUDES.

I.—LIFE OF LIFE

What's that, which, ere I spake, was gone?
So joyful and intense a spark
That, whilst o'erhead the wonder shone,

The day, before but dull, grew dark.
I do not know; but this I know,
That, had the splendour lived a year,
The truth that I some heavenly show
Did see, could not be now more clear.
This know I too: might mortal breath
Express the passion then inspired,
Evil would die a natural death,
And nothing transient be desired;
And error from the soul would pass,
And leave the senses pure and strong
As sunbeams. But the best, alas,
Has neither memory nor tongue!

II.—THE REVELATION.

An idle poet, here and there,
Looks round him; but, for all the rest,
The world, unfathomably fair,
Is duller than a witling's jest.
Love wakes men, once a lifetime each;
They lift their heavy lids, and look;
And, lo, what one sweet page can teach,
They read with joy, then shut the book.
And some give thanks, and some blaspheme,
And most forget; but, either way,
That and the Child's unheeded dream
Is all the light of all their day.

III.—THE SPIRIT'S EPOCHS.

Not in the crises of events,
Of compass'd hopes, or fears fulfill'd,
Or acts of gravest consequence,
Are life's delight and depth reveal'd.
The day of days was not the day;
That went before, or was postponed;
The night Death took our lamp away
Was not the night on which we groan'd.
I drew my bride, beneath the moon,
Across my threshold; happy hour!
But, ah, the walk that afternoon
We saw the water-flags in flower!

IV.—THE PROTOTYPE.

Lo, there, whence love, life, light are pour'd,

Veil'd with impenetrable rays,
Amidst the presence of the Lord
Co-equal Wisdom laughs and plays.
Female and male God made the man;
His image is the whole, not half;
And in our love we dimly scan
The love which is between Himself.

V.—THE PRAISE OF LOVE.

Spirit of Knowledge, grant me this:
A simple heart and subtle wit
To praise the thing whose praise it is
That all which can be praised is it.

SARUM PLAIN.

1

Breakfast enjoy'd, 'mid hush of boughs
And perfumes thro' the windows blown;
Brief worship done, which still endows
The day with beauty not its own;
With intervening pause, that paints
Each act with honour, life with calm
(As old processions of the Saints
At every step have wands of palm),
We rose; the ladies went to dress,
And soon return'd with smiles; and then,
Plans fix'd, to which the Dean said 'Yes,'
Once more we drove to Salisbury Plain.
We past my house (observed with praise
By Mildred, Mary acquiesced),
And left the old and lazy greys
Below the hill, and walk'd the rest.

2

The moods of love are like the wind,
And none knows whence or why they rise:
I ne'er before felt heart and mind
So much affected through mine eyes.
How cognate with the flatter'd air,
How form'd for earth's familiar zone,
She moved; how feeling and how fair
For others' pleasure and her own!
And, ah, the heaven of her face!
How, when she laugh'd, I seem'd to see

The gladness of the primal grace,
And how, when grave, its dignity!
Of all she was, the least not less
Delighted the devoted eye;
No fold or fashion of her dress
Her fairness did not sanctify.
I could not else than grieve. What cause?
Was I not blest? Was she not there?
Likely my own? Ah, that it was:
How like seem'd 'likely' to despair!

3

And yet to see her so benign,
So honourable and womanly,
In every maiden kindness mine,
And full of gayest courtesy,
Was pleasure so without alloy,
Such unreproved, sufficient bliss,
I almost wish'd, the while, that joy
Might never further go than this.
So much it was as now to walk,
And humbly by her gentle side
Observe her smile and hear her talk,
Could it be more to call her Bride?
I feign'd her won: the mind finite,
Puzzled and fagg'd by stress and strain
To comprehend the whole delight,
Made bliss more hard to bear than pain.
All good, save heart to hold, so summ'd
And grasp'd, the thought smote, like a knife,
How laps'd mortality had numb'd
The feelings to the feast of life;
How passing good breathes sweetest breath;
And love itself at highest reveals
More black than bright, commending death
By teaching how much life conceals.

4

But happier passions these subdued,
When from the close and sultry lane,
With eyes made bright by what they view'd,
We emerged upon the mounded Plain.
As to the breeze a flag unfurls,
My spirit expanded, sweetly embraced
By those same gusts that shook her curls
And vex'd the ribbon at her waist.

To the future cast I future cares;
Breathed with a heart unfreighted, free,
And laugh'd at the presumptuous airs
That with her muslins folded me;
Till, one vague rack along my sky,
The thought that she might ne'er be mine
Lay half forgotten by the eye
So feasted with the sun's warm shine.

5

By the great stones we chose our ground
For shade; and there, in converse sweet,
Took luncheon. On a little mound
Sat the three ladies; at their feet
I sat; and smelt the heathy smell,
Pluck'd harebells, turn'd the telescope
To the country round. My life went well,
For once, without the wheels of hope;
And I despised the Druid rocks
That scowl'd their chill gloom from above,
Like churls whose stolid wisdom mocks
The lightness of immortal love.
And, as we talk'd, my spirit quaff'd
The sparkling winds; the candid skies
At our untruthful strangeness laugh'd;
I kiss'd with mine her smiling eyes;
And sweet familiarness and awe
Prevail'd that hour on either part,
And in the eternal light I saw
That she was mine; though yet my heart
Could not conceive, nor would confess
Such contentation; and there grew
More form and more fair stateliness
Than heretofore between us two.

CANTO IX.—SAHARA

PRELUDES.

I.—THE WIFE'S TRAGEDY

Man must be pleased; but him to please
Is woman's pleasure; down the gulf
Of his condoled necessities
She casts her best, she flings herself.

34

How often flings for nought, and yokes
Her heart to an icicle or whim,
Whose each impatient word provokes
Another, not from her, but him;
While she, too gentle even to force
His penitence by kind replies,
Waits by, expecting his remorse,
With pardon in her pitying eyes;
And if he once, by shame oppress'd,
A comfortable word confers,
She leans and weeps against his breast,
And seems to think the sin was hers;
And whilst his love has any life,
Or any eye to see her charms,
At any time, she's still his wife,
Dearly devoted to his arms;
She loves with love that cannot tire;
And when, ah woe, she loves alone,
Through passionate duty love springs higher,
As grass grows taller round a stone.

II.—COMMON GRACES.

Is nature in thee too spiritless,
Ignoble, impotent, and dead,
To prize her love and loveliness
The more for being thy daily bread?
And art thou one of that vile crew
Which see no splendour in the sun,
Praising alone the good that's new,
Or over, or not yet begun?
And has it dawn'd on thy dull wits
That love warms many as soft a nest,
That, though swathed round with benefits,
Thou art not singularly blest?
And fail thy thanks for gifts divine,
The common food of many a heart,
Because they are not only thine?
Beware lest in the end thou art
Cast for thy pride forth from the fold,
Too good to feel the common grace
Of blissful myriads who behold
For evermore the Father's face.

III.—THE ZEST OF LIFE.

Give thanks. It is not time misspent;

35

Worst fare this betters, and the best,
Wanting this natural condiment,
Breeds crudeness, and will not digest.
The grateful love the Giver's law;
But those who eat, and look no higher,
From sin or doubtful sanction draw
The biting sauce their feasts require.
Give thanks for nought, if you've no more,
And, having all things, do not doubt
That nought, with thanks, is blest before
Whate'er the world can give, without.

IV.—FOOL AND WISE.

Endow the fool with sun and moon,
Being his, he holds them mean and low,
But to the wise a little boon
Is great, because the giver's so.

SAHARA.

1

I stood by Honor and the Dean,
They seated in the London train.
A month from her! yet this had been,
Ere now, without such bitter pain.
But neighbourhood makes parting light,
And distance remedy has none;
Alone, she near, I felt as might
A blind man sitting in the sun;
She near, all for the time was well;
Hope's self, when we were far apart,
With lonely feeling, like the smell
Of heath on mountains, fill'd my heart.
To see her seem'd delight's full scope,
And her kind smile, so clear of care,
Ev'n then, though darkening all my hope,
Gilded the cloud of my despair.

2

She had forgot to bring a book.
I lent one; blamed the print for old;
And did not tell her that she took
A Petrarch worth its weight in gold.
I hoped she'd lose it; for my love
Was grown so dainty, high, and nice,

It prized no luxury above
The sense of fruitless sacrifice.

3

The bell rang, and, with shrieks like death,
Link catching link, the long array,
With ponderous pulse and fiery breath,
Proud of its burthen, swept away;
And through the lingering crowd I broke,
Sought the hill-side, and thence, heart-sick,
Beheld, far off, the little smoke
Along the landscape kindling quick.

4

What should I do, where should I go,
Now she was gone, my love! for mine
She was, whatever here below
Cross'd or usurp'd my right divine.
Life, without her, was vain and gross,
The glory from the world was gone,
And on the gardens of the Close
As on Sahara shone the sun.
Oppress'd with her departed grace,
My thoughts on ill surmises fed;
The harmful influence of the place
She went to fill'd my soul with dread.
She, mixing with the people there,
Might come back alter'd, having caught
The foolish, fashionable air
Of knowing all, and feeling nought.
Or, giddy with her beauty's praise,
She'd scorn our simple country life,
Its wholesome nights and tranquil days.
And would not deign to be my Wife.
'My Wife,' 'my Wife,' ah, tenderest word!
How oft, as fearful she might hear,
Whispering that name of 'Wife,' I heard
The chiming of the inmost sphere.

5

I pass'd the home of my regret.
The clock was striking in the hall,
And one sad window open yet,
Although the dews began to fall.
Ah, distance show'd her beauty's scope!
How light of heart and innocent

That loveliness which sicken'd hope
And wore the world for ornament!
How perfectly her life was framed;
And, thought of in that passionate mood,
How her affecting graces shamed
The vulgar life that was but good!

6

I wonder'd, would her bird be fed,
Her rose-plots water'd, she not by;
Loading my breast with angry dread
Of light, unlikely injury.
So, fill'd with love and fond remorse,
I paced the Close, its every part
Endow'd with reliquary force
To heal and raise from death my heart.
How tranquil and unsecular
The precinct! Once, through yonder gate,
I saw her go, and knew from far
Her love-lit form and gentle state.
Her dress had brush'd this wicket; here
She turn'd her face, and laugh'd, with light
Like moonbeams on a wavering mere.
Weary beforehand of the night,
I went; the blackbird, in the wood
Talk'd by himself, and eastward grew
In heaven the symbol of my mood,
Where one bright star engross'd the blue.

CANTO X—CHURCH TO CHURCH

PRELUDES.

I.—THE JOYFUL WISDOM

Would Wisdom for herself be woo'd,
And wake the foolish from his dream,
She must be glad as well as good,
And must not only be, but seem.
Beauty and joy are hers by right;
And, knowing this, I wonder less
That she's so scorn'd, when falsely dight
In misery and ugliness.
What's that which Heaven to man endears,
And that which eyes no sooner see

Than the heart says, with floods of tears,
'Ah, that's the thing which I would be!'
Not childhood, full of frown and fret;
Not youth, impatient to disown
Those visions high, which to forget
Were worse than never to have known;
Not worldlings, in whose fair outside
Nor courtesy nor justice fails,
Thanks to cross-pulling vices tied,
Like Samson's foxes, by the tails;
Not poets; real things are dreams,
When dreams are as realities,
And boasters of celestial gleams
Go stumbling aye for want of eyes;
Not patriots or people's men,
In whom two worse-match'd evils meet
Than ever sought Adullam's den,
Base conscience and a high conceit;
Not new-made saints, their feelings iced,
Their joy in man and nature gone,
Who sing 'O easy yoke of Christ!'
But find 'tis hard to get it on;
Not great men, even when they're good;
The good man whom the time makes great,
By some disgrace of chance or blood,
God fails not to humiliate;
Not these: but souls, found here and there,
Oases in our waste of sin,
Where everything is well and fair,
And Heav'n remits its discipline;
Whose sweet subdual of the world
The worldling scarce can recognise,
And ridicule, against it hurl'd,
Drops with a broken sting and dies;
Who nobly, if they cannot know
Whether a 'scutcheon's dubious field
Carries a falcon or a crow,
Fancy a falcon on the shield;
Yet, ever careful not to hurt
God's honour, who creates success,
Their praise of even the best desert
Is but to have presumed no less;
Who, should their own life plaudits bring,
Are simply vex'd at heart that such
An easy, yea, delightful thing
Should move the minds of men so much.

39

They live by law, not like the fool,
But like the bard, who freely sings
In strictest bonds of rhyme and rule,
And finds in them, not bonds, but wings.
Postponing still their private ease
To courtly custom, appetite,
Subjected to observances,
To banquet goes with full delight;
Nay, continence and gratitude
So cleanse their lives from earth's alloy,
They taste, in Nature's common food,
Nothing but spiritual joy.
They shine like Moses in the face,
And teach our hearts, without the rod,
That God's grace is the only grace,
And all grace is the grace of God.

II.—THE DEVICES.

Love, kiss'd by Wisdom, wakes twice Love,
And Wisdom is, thro' loving, wise.
Let Dove and Snake, and Snake and Dove,
This Wisdom's be, that Love's device.

GOING TO CHURCH.

1

I woke at three; for I was bid
To breakfast with the Dean at nine,
And thence to Church. My curtain slid,
I found the dawning Sunday fine,
And could not rest, so rose. The air
Was dark and sharp; the roosted birds
Cheep'd, 'Here am I, Sweet; are you there?'
On Avon's misty flats the herds
Expected, comfortless, the day,
Which slowly fired the clouds above;
The cock scream'd, somewhere far away;
In sleep the matrimonial dove
Was crooning; no wind waked the wood,
Nor moved the midnight river-damps,
Nor thrill'd the poplar; quiet stood
The chestnut with its thousand lamps;
The moon shone yet, but weak and drear,
And seem'd to watch, with bated breath,
The landscape, all made sharp and clear

By stillness, as a face by death.

2

My pray'rs for her being done, I took
Occasion by the quiet hour
To find and know, by Rule and Book,
The rights of love's beloved power.

3

Fronting the question without ruth,
Nor ignorant that, evermore,
If men will stoop to kiss the Truth,
She lifts them higher than before,
I, from above, such light required
As now should once for all destroy
The folly which at times desired
A sanction for so great a joy.

4

Thenceforth, and through that pray'r, I trod
A path with no suspicions dim.
I loved her in the name of God,
And for the ray she was of Him;
I ought to admire much more, not less
Her beauty was a godly grace;
The mystery of loveliness,
Which made an altar of her face,
Was not of the flesh, though that was fair,
But a most pure and living light
Without a name, by which the rare
And virtuous spirit flamed to sight.
If oft, in love, effect lack'd cause
And cause effect, 'twere vain to soar
Reasons to seek for that which was
Reason itself, or something more.
My joy was no idolatry
Upon the ends of the vile earth bent,
For when I loved her most then I
Most yearn'd for more divine content.
That other doubt, which, like a ghost,
In the brain's darkness haunted me,
Was thus resolved: Him loved I most,
But her I loved most sensibly.
Lastly, my giddiest hope allow'd
No selfish thought, or earthly smirch;
And forth I went, in peace, and proud

41

To take my passion into Church;
Grateful and glad to think that all
Such doubts would seem entirely vain
To her whose nature's lighter fall
Made no divorce of heart from brain.

5

I found them, with exactest grace
And fresh as Spring, for Spring attired;
And by the radiance in her face
I saw she felt she was admired;
And, through the common luck of love,
A moment's fortunate delay,
To fit the little lilac glove,
Gave me her arm; and I and they
(They true to this and every hour,
As if attended on by Time),
Enter'd the Church while yet the tower
Was noisy with the finish'd chime.

6

Her soft voice, singularly heard
Beside me, in her chant, withstood
The roar of voices, like a bird
Sole warbling in a windy wood;
And, when we knelt, she seem'd to be
An angel teaching me to pray;
And all through the high Liturgy
My spirit rejoiced without allay,
Being, for once, borne clearly above
All banks and bars of ignorance,
By this bright spring-tide of pure love,
And floated in a free expanse,
Whence it could see from side to side,
The obscurity from every part
Winnow'd away and purified
By the vibrations of my heart.

CANTO XI.—THE DANCE

PRELUDES.

I.—THE DAUGHTER OF EVE.

The woman's gentle mood o'erstept
Withers my love, that lightly scans

42

The rest, and does in her accept
All her own faults, but none of man's.
As man I cannot judge her ill,
Or honour her fair station less,
Who, with a woman's errors, still
Preserves a woman's gentleness;
For thus I think, if one I see
Who disappoints my high desire,
'How admirable would she be,
Could she but know how I admire!'
Or fail she, though from blemish clear,
To charm, I call it my defect;
And so my thought, with reverent fear
To err by doltish disrespect,
Imputes love's great regard, and says,
'Though unapparent 'tis to me,
Be sure this Queen some other sways
With well-perceiv'd supremacy.'
Behold the worst! Light from above
On the blank ruin writes 'Forbear!
Her first crime was unguarded love,
And all the rest, perhaps, despair.'
Discrown'd, dejected, but not lost,
O, sad one, with no more a name
Or place in all the honour'd host
Of maiden and of matron fame,
Grieve on; but, if thou grievest right,
'Tis not that these abhor thy state,
Nor would'st thou lower the least the height
Which makes thy casting down so great.
Good is thy lot in its degree;
For hearts that verily repent
Are burden'd with impunity
And comforted by chastisement.
Sweet patience sanctify thy woes!
And doubt not but our God is just,
Albeit unscathed thy traitor goes,
And thou art stricken to the dust.
That penalty's the best to bear
Which follows soonest on the sin;
And guilt's a game where losers fare
Better than those who seem to win.

II.—AUREA DICTA.

'Tis truth (although this truth's a star

Too deep-enskied for all to see),
As poets of grammar, lovers are
The fountains of morality.

Child, would you shun the vulgar doom,
In love disgust, in death despair?
Know, death must come and love must come,
And so for each your soul prepare.

Who pleasure follows pleasure slays;
God's wrath upon himself he wreaks;
But all delights rejoice his days
Who takes with thanks, and never seeks.

The wrong is made and measured by
The right's inverted dignity.
Change love to shame, as love is high
So low in hell your bed shall be.

How easy to keep free from sin!
How hard that freedom to recall!
For dreadful truth it is that men
Forget the heavens from which they fall.

Lest sacred love your soul ensnare,
With pious fancy still infer
'How loving and how lovely fair
Must He be who has fashion'd her!'

Become whatever good you see,
Nor sigh if, forthwith, fades from view
The grace of which you may not be
The subject and spectator too.

Love's perfect blossom only blows
Where noble manners veil defect
Angels maybe familiar; those
Who err each other must respect.

Love blabb'd of is a great decline;
A careless word unsanctions sense;
But he who casts Heaven's truth to swine
Consummates all incontinence.

Not to unveil before the gaze
Of an imperfect sympathy
In aught we are, is the sweet praise
And the main sum of modesty.

THE DANCE.

1

'My memory of Heaven awakes!
She's not of the earth, although her light,
As lantern'd by her body, makes
A piece of it past bearing bright.
So innocently proud and fair
She is, that Wisdom sings for glee
And Folly dies, breathing one air
With such a bright-cheek'd chastity;
And though her charms are a strong law
Compelling all men to admire,
They go so clad with lovely awe
None but the noble dares desire.
He who would seek to make her his
Will comprehend that souls of grace
Own sweet repulsion, and that 'tis
The quality of their embrace
To be like the majestic reach
Of coupled suns, that, from afar,
Mingle their mutual spheres, while each
Circles the twin obsequious star;
And, in the warmth of hand to hand,
Of heart to heart, he'll vow to note
And reverently understand
How the two spirits shine remote;
And ne'er to numb fine honour's nerve,
Nor let sweet awe in passion melt,
Nor fail by courtesies to observe
The space which makes attraction felt;
Nor cease to guard like life the sense
Which tells him that the embrace of love
Is o'er a gulf of difference
Love cannot sound, nor death remove.'

2

This learn'd I, watching where she danced,
Native to melody and light,
And now and then toward me glanced,
Pleased, as I hoped, to please my sight.

3

Ah, love to speak was impotent,
Till music did a tongue confer,
And I ne'er knew what music meant,

45

Until I danced to it with her.
Too proud of the sustaining power
Of my, till then, unblemish'd joy.
My passion, for reproof, that hour
Tasted mortality's alloy,
And bore me down an eddying gulf;
I wish'd the world might run to wreck,
So I but once might fling myself
Obliviously about her neck.
I press'd her hand, by will or chance
I know not, but I saw the rays
Withdrawn, which did till then enhance
Her fairness with its thanks for praise.
I knew my spirit's vague offence
Was patent to the dreaming eye
And heavenly tact of innocence,
And did for fear my fear defy,
And ask'd her for the next dance. 'Yes.'
'No,' had not fall'n with half the force.
She was fulfill'd with gentleness,
And I with measureless remorse;
And, ere I slept, on bended knee
I own'd myself, with many a tear,
Unseasonable, disorderly,
And a deranger of love's sphere;
Gave thanks that, when we stumble and fall,
We hurt ourselves, and not the truth;
And, rising, found its brightness all
The brighter through the tears of ruth.

4

Nor was my hope that night made less,
Though order'd, humbled, and reproved;
Her farewell did her heart express
As much, but not with anger, moved.
My trouble had my soul betray'd;
And, in the night of my despair,
My love, a flower of noon afraid,
Divulged its fulness unaware.
I saw she saw; and, O sweet Heaven,
Could my glad mind have credited
That influence had to me been given
To affect her so, I should have said
That, though she from herself conceal'd
Love's felt delight and fancied harm,
They made her face the jousting field

46

Of joy and beautiful alarm.

CANTO XII—THE ABDICATION.

PRELUDES.

I.—THE CHACE.

She wearies with an ill unknown;
In sleep she sobs and seems to float,
A water-lily, all alone
Within a lonely castle-moat;
And as the full-moon, spectral, lies
Within the crescent's gleaming arms,
The present shows her heedless eyes
A future dim with vague alarms.
She sees, and yet she scarcely sees,
For, life-in-life not yet begun,
Too many are its mysteries
For thought to fix on any one.
She's told that maidens are by youths
Extremely honour'd and desired;
And sighs, 'If those sweet tales be truths,
What bliss to be so much admired!'
The suitors come; she sees them grieve;
Her coldness fills them with despair;
She'd pity if she could believe;
She's sorry that she cannot care.
But who now meets her on her way?
Comes he as enemy or friend,
Or both? Her bosom seems to say,
He cannot pass, and there an end.
Whom does he love? Does he confer
His heart on worth that answers his?
Or is he come to worship her?
She fears, she hopes, she thinks he is!
Advancing stepless, quick, and still,
As in the grass a serpent glides,
He fascinates her fluttering will,
Then terrifies with dreadful strides.
At first, there's nothing to resist;
He fights with all the forms of peace;
He comes about her like a mist,
With subtle, swift, unseen increase;
And then, unlook'd for, strikes amain

47

Some stroke that frightens her to death,
And grows all harmlessness again,
Ere she can cry, or get her breath.
At times she stops, and stands at bay;
But he, in all more strong than she,
Subdues her with his pale dismay,
Or more admired audacity.
She plans some final, fatal blow,
But when she means with frowns to kill,
He looks as if he loved her so,
She smiles to him against her will.
How sweetly he implies her praise!
His tender talk, his gentle tone,
The manly worship in his gaze,
They nearly make her heart his own.
With what an air he speaks her name;
His manner always recollects
Her sex, and still the woman's claim
Is taught its scope by his respects.
Her charms, perceived to prosper first
In his beloved advertencies,
When in her glass they are rehearsed,
Prove his most powerful allies.
Ah, whither shall a maiden flee,
When a bold youth so swift pursues,
And siege of tenderest courtesy,
With hope perseverant, still renews!
Why fly so fast? Her flatter'd breast
Thanks him who finds her fair and good;
She loves her fears; veil'd joys arrest
The foolish terrors of her blood;
By secret, sweet degrees, her heart,
Vanquish'd, takes warmth from his desire;
She makes it more, with hidden art,
And fuels love's late dreaded fire.
The generous credit he accords
To all the signs of good in her
Redeems itself; his praiseful words
The virtues they impute confer.
Her heart is thrice as rich in bliss,
She's three times gentler than before;
He gains a right to call her his,
Now she through him is so much more;
'Tis heaven where'er she turns her head;
'Tis music when she talks; 'tis air
On which, elate, she seems to tread,

The convert of a gladder sphere!
Ah, might he, when by doubts aggrieved,
Behold his tokens next her breast,
At all his words and sighs perceived
Against its blythe upheaval press'd!
But still she flies. Should she be won,
It must not be believed or thought
She yields; she's chased to death, undone,
Surprised, and violently caught.

II.—DENIED.

The storm-cloud, whose portentous shade
Fumes from a core of smother'd fire,
His livery is whose worshipp'd maid
Denies herself to his desire.
Ah, grief that almost crushes life,
To lie upon his lonely bed,
And fancy her another's wife!
His brain is flame, his heart is lead.
Sinking at last, by nature's course,
Cloak'd round with sleep from his despair,
He does but sleep to gather force
That goes to his exhausted care.
He wakes renew'd for all the smart.
His only Love, and she is wed!
His fondness comes about his heart,
As milk comes, when the babe is dead.
The wretch, whom she found fit for scorn,
His own allegiant thoughts despise;
And far into the shining morn
Lazy with misery he lies.

III.—THE CHURL.

This marks the Churl: when spousals crown
His selfish hope, he finds the grace,
Which sweet love has for ev'n the clown,
Was not in the woman, but the chace.

THE ABDICATION.

1

From little signs, like little stars,
Whose faint impression on the sense
The very looking straight at mars,
Or only seen by confluence;

49

From instinct of a mutual thought,
Whence sanctity of manners flow'd;
From chance unconscious, and from what
Concealment, overconscious, show'd;
Her hand's less weight upon my arm,
Her lowlier mien; that match'd with this;
I found, and felt with strange alarm
I stood committed to my bliss.

2

I grew assured, before I ask'd,
That she'd be mine without reserve,
And in her unclaim'd graces bask'd,
At leisure, till the time should serve,
With just enough of dread to thrill
The hope, and make it trebly dear;
Thus loth to speak the word to kill
Either the hope or happy fear.

3

Till once, through lanes returning late,
Her laughing sisters lagg'd behind;
And, ere we reach'd her father's gate,
We paused with one presentient mind;
And, in the dim and perfumed mist,
Their coming stay'd, who, friends to me,
And very women, loved to assist
Love's timid opportunity.

4

Twice rose, twice died my trembling word;
The faint and frail Cathedral chimes
Spake time in music, and we heard
The chafers rustling in the limes.
Her dress, that touch'd me where I stood,
The warmth of her confided arm,
Her bosom's gentle neighbourhood,
Her pleasure in her power to charm;
Her look, her love, her form, her touch,
The least seem'd most by blissful turn,
Blissful but that it pleased too much,
And taught the wayward soul to yearn.
It was as if a harp with wires
Was traversed by the breath I drew;
And, oh, sweet meeting of desires,
She, answering, own'd that she loved too.

5

Honoria was to be my bride!
The hopeless heights of hope were scaled
The summit won, I paused and sigh'd,
As if success itself had fail'd.
It seem'd as if my lips approach'd
To touch at Tantalus' reward,
And rashly on Eden life encroach'd,
Half-blinded by the flaming sword.
The whole world's wealthiest and its best,
So fiercely sought, appear'd when found,
Poor in its need to be possess'd,
Poor from its very want of bound.
My queen was crouching at my side,
By love unsceptred and brought low,
Her awful garb of maiden pride
All melted into tears like snow;
The mistress of my reverent thought,
Whose praise was all I ask'd of fame,
In my close-watch'd approval sought
Protection as from danger and blame;
Her soul, which late I loved to invest
With pity for my poor desert,
Buried its face within my breast,
Like a pet fawn by hunters hurt.

BOOK II

THE PROLOGUE.

1

Her sons pursue the butterflies,
Her baby daughter mocks the doves
With throbbing coo; in his fond eyes
She's Venus with her little Loves;
Her footfall dignifies the earth,
Her form's the native-land of grace,
And, lo, his coming lights with mirth
Its court and capital her face!
Full proud her favour makes her lord,
And that her flatter'd bosom knows.
She takes his arm without a word,
In lanes of laurel and of rose.
Ten years to-day has she been his.

He but begins to understand,
He says, the dignity and bliss
She gave him when she gave her hand.
She, answering, says, he disenchants
The past, though that was perfect; he
Rejoins, the present nothing wants
But briefness to be ecstasy.
He lands her charms; her beauty's glow
Wins from the spoiler Time new rays;
Bright looks reply, approving so
Beauty's elixir vitae, praise.
Upon a beech he bids her mark
Where, ten years since, he carved her name;
It grows there with the growing bark,
And in his heart it grows the same.
For that her soft arm presses his
Close to her fond, maternal breast;
He tells her, each new kindness is
The effectual sum of all the rest!
And, whilst the cushat, mocking, coo'd,
They blest the days they had been wed,
At cost of those in which he woo'd,
Till everything was three times said;
And words were growing vain, when Briggs,
Factotum, Footman, Butler, Groom,
Who press'd the cyder, fed the pigs,
Preserv'd the rabbits, drove the brougham,
And help'd, at need, to mow the lawns,
And sweep the paths and thatch the hay,
Here brought the Post down, Mrs. Vaughan's
Sole rival, but, for once, to-day,
Scarce look'd at; for the 'Second Book,'
Till this tenth festival kept close,
Was thus commenced, while o'er them shook
The laurel married with the rose.

2

'The pulse of War, whose bloody heats
Sane purposes insanely work,
Now with fraternal frenzy beats,
And binds the Christian to the Turk,
And shrieking fifes' -

3

But, with a roar,
In rush'd the Loves; the tallest roll'd

A hedgehog from his pinafore,
Which saved his fingers; Baby, bold,
Touch'd it, and stared, and scream'd for life,
And stretch'd her hand for Vaughan to kiss,
Who hugg'd his Pet, and ask'd his wife,
'Is this for love, or love for this?'
But she turn'd pale, for, lo, the beast,
Found stock-still in the rabbit-trap,
And feigning so to be deceased,
And laid by Frank upon her lap,
Unglobed himself, and show'd his snout,
And fell, scatt'ring the Loves amain,
With shriek, with laughter, and with shout;
And, peace at last restored again,
The bard, who this untimely hitch
Bore with a calm magnanimous,
(The hedgehog rolled into a ditch,
And Venus sooth'd), proceeded thus:

CANTO I.—ACCEPTED

PRELUDES.

I.—THE SONG OF SONGS.

The pulse of War, whose bloody heats
Sane purposes insanely work,
Now with fraternal frenzy beats,
And binds the Christian to the Turk,
And shrieking fifes and braggart flags,
Through quiet England, teach our breath
The courage corporate that drags
The coward to heroic death.
Too late for song! Who henceforth sings,
Must fledge his heavenly flight with more
Song-worthy and heroic things
Than hasty, home-destroying war.
While might and right are not agreed,
And battle thus is yet to wage,
So long let laurels be the meed
Of soldier as of poet sage;
But men expect the Tale of Love,
And weary of the Tale of Hate;
Lift me, O Muse, myself above,
And let the world no longer wait!

53

II.—THE KITES.

I saw three Cupids (so I dream'd),
Who made three kites, on which were drawn,
In letters that like roses gleam'd,
'Plato,' 'Anacreon,' and 'Vaughan.'
The boy who held by Plato tried
His airy venture first; all sail,
It heav'nward rush'd till scarce descried,
Then pitch'd and dropp'd for want of tail.
Anacreon's Love, with shouts of mirth
That pride of spirit thus should fall,
To his kite link'd a lump of earth,
And, lo, it would not soar at all.
Last, my disciple freighted his
With a long streamer made of flowers,
The children of the sod, and this
Rose in the sun, and flew for hours.

III.—ORPHEUS.

The music of the Sirens found
Ulysses weak, though cords were strong;
But happier Orpheus stood unbound,
And shamed it with a sweeter song.
His mode be mine. Of Heav'n I ask,
May I, with heart-persuading might,
Pursue the Poet's sacred task
Of superseding faith by sight,
Till ev'n the witless Gadarene,
Preferring Christ to swine, shall know
That life is sweetest when it's clean.
To prouder folly let me show
Earth by divine light made divine;
And let the saints, who hear my word,
Say, 'Lo, the clouds begin to shine
About the coming of the Lord!'

IV.—NEAREST THE DEAREST.

Till Eve was brought to Adam, he
A solitary desert trod,
Though in the great society
Of nature, angels, and of God.
If one slight column counterweighs
The ocean, 'tis the Maker's law,
Who deems obedience better praise
Than sacrifice of erring awe.

54

V.—PERSPECTIVE.

What seems to us for us is true.
The planet has no proper light,
And yet, when Venus is in view,
No primal star is half so bright.

ACCEPTED.

1

What fortune did my heart foretell?
What shook my spirit, as I woke,
Like the vibration of a bell
Of which I had not heard the stroke?
Was it some happy vision shut
From memory by the sun's fresh ray?
Was it that linnet's song; or but
A natural gratitude for day?
Or the mere joy the senses weave,
A wayward ecstasy of life?
Then I remember'd, yester-eve
I won Honoria for my Wife.

2

Forth riding, while as yet the day
Was dewy, watching Sarum Spire,
Still beckoning me along my way,
And growing every minute higher,
I reach'd the Dean's. One blind was down,
Though nine then struck. My bride to be!
And had she rested ill, my own,
With thinking (oh, my heart!) of me?
I paced the streets; a pistol chose,
To guard my now important life
When riding late from Sarum Close;
At noon return'd. Good Mrs. Fife,
To my, 'The Dean, is he at home?'
Said, 'No, sir; but Miss Honor is;'
And straight, not asking if I'd come,
Announced me, 'Mr. Felix, Miss,'
To Mildred, in the Study. There
We talk'd, she working. We agreed
The day was fine; the Fancy-Fair
Successful; 'Did I ever read
De Genlis?' 'Never.' 'Do! She heard
I was engaged.' 'To whom?' 'Miss Fry
Was it the fact?' 'No!' 'On my word?'

'What scandal people talk'd!' 'Would I
Hold out this skein of silk.' So pass'd
I knew not how much time away.
'How were her sisters?' 'Well.' At last
I summon'd heart enough to say,
'I hoped to have seen Miss Churchill too.'
'Miss Churchill, Felix! What is this?
I said, and now I find 'tis true,
Last night you quarrell'd! Here she is.'

3

She came, and seem'd a morning rose
When ruffling rain has paled its blush;
Her crown once more was on her brows;
And, with a faint, indignant flush,
And fainter smile, she gave her hand,
But not her eyes, then sate apart,
As if to make me understand
The honour of her vanquish'd heart.
But I drew humbly to her side;
And she, well pleased, perceiving me
Liege ever to the noble pride
Of her unconquer'd majesty,
Once and for all put it away;
The faint flush pass'd; and, thereupon,
Her loveliness, which rather lay
In light than colour, smiled and shone,
Till sick was all my soul with bliss;
Or was it with remorse and ire
Of such a sanctity as this
Subdued by love to my desire?

CANTO II.—THE COURSE OF TRUE LOVE.

PRELUDES.

I.—THE CHANGED ALLEGIANCE.

Watch how a bird, that captived sings,
The cage set open, first looks out,
Yet fears the freedom of his wings,
And now withdraws, and flits about,
And now looks forth again; until,
Grown bold, he hops on stool and chair,
And now attains the window-sill,

And now confides himself to air.
The maiden so, from love's free sky
In chaste and prudent counsels caged,
But longing to be loosen'd by
Her suitor's faith declared and gaged,
When blest with that release desired,
First doubts if truly she is free,
Then pauses, restlessly retired,
Alarm'd at too much liberty;
But soon, remembering all her debt
To plighted passion, gets by rote
Her duty; says, 'I love him!' yet
The thought half chokes her in her throat;
And, like that fatal 'I am thine,'
Comes with alternate gush and check
And joltings of the heart, as wine
Pour'd from a flask of narrow neck.
Is he indeed her choice? She fears
Her Yes was rashly said, and shame,
Remorse and ineffectual tears
Revolt from has conceded claim.
Oh, treason! So, with desperate nerve,
She cries, 'I am in love, am his;'
Lets run the cables of reserve,
And floats into a sea of bliss,
And laughs to think of her alarm,
Avows she was in love before,
Though has avowal was the charm
Which open'd to her own the door.
She loves him for his mastering air,
Whence, Parthian-like, she slaying flies;
His flattering look, which seems to wear
Her loveliness in manly eyes;
His smile, which, by reverse, portends
An awful wrath, should reason stir;
(How fortunate it is they're friends,
And he will ne'er be wroth with her!)
His power to do or guard from harm;
If he but chose to use it half,
And catch her up in one strong arm,
What could she do but weep, or laugh!
His words, which still instruct, but so
That this applause seems still implied,
'How wise in all she ought to know,
How ignorant of all beside!'
His skilful suit, which leaves her free,

57

Gives nothing for the world to name,
And keeps her conscience safe, while he,
With half the bliss, takes all the blame;
His clear repute with great and small;
The jealousy his choice will stir;
But ten times more than ten times all,
She loves him for his love of her.
How happy 'tis he seems to see
In her that utter loveliness
Which she, for his sake, longs to be!
At times, she cannot but confess
Her other friends are somewhat blind;
Her parents' years excuse neglect,
But all the rest are scarcely kind,
And brothers grossly want respect;
And oft she views what he admires
Within her glass, and sight of this
Makes all the sum of her desires
To be devotion unto his.
But still, at first, whatever's done,
A touch, her hand press'd lightly, she
Stands dizzied, shock'd, and flush'd, like one
Set sudden neck-deep in the sea;
And, though her bond for endless time
To his good pleasure gives her o'er,
The slightest favour seems a crime,
Because it makes her love him more.
But that she ne'er will let him know;
For what were love should reverence cease?
A thought which makes her reason so
Inscrutable, it seems caprice.
With her, as with a desperate town,
Too weak to stand, too proud to treat,
The conqueror, though the walls are down,
Has still to capture street by street;
But, after that, habitual faith,
Divorced from self, where late 'twas due,
Walks nobly in its novel path,
And she's to changed allegiance true;
And prizing what she can't prevent,
(Right wisdom, often misdeem'd whim),
Her will's indomitably bent
On mere submissiveness to him;
To him she'll cleave, for him forsake
Father's and mother's fond command!
He is her lord, for he can take

58

Hold of her faint heart with his hand.

II.—BEAUTY.

'Beauty deludes.' O shaft well shot,
To strike the mark's true opposite!
That ugly good is scorn'd proves not
'Tis beauty lies, but lack of it.
By Heaven's law the Jew might take
A slave to wife, if she was fair;
So strong a plea does beauty make
That, where 'tis seen, discretion's there.
If, by a monstrous chance, we learn
That this illustrious vaunt's a lie,
Our minds, by which the eyes discern,
See hideous contrariety.
And laugh at Nature's wanton mood,
Which, thus a swinish thing to flout,
Though haply in its gross way good,
Hangs such a jewel in its snout.

III.—LAIS AND LUCRETIA.

Did first his beauty wake her sighs?
That's Lais! Thus Lucretia's known:
The beauty in her Lover's eyes
Was admiration of her own.

THE COURSE OF TRUE LOVE.

1

Oh, beating heart of sweet alarm,
Which stays the lover's step, when near
His mistress and her awful charm
Of grace and innocence sincere!
I held the half-shut door, and heard
The voice of my betrothed wife,
Who sang my verses, every word
By music taught its latent life;
With interludes of well-touch'd notes,
That flash'd, surprising and serene,
As meteor after meteor floats
The soft, autumnal stars between.
There was a passion in her tone,
A tremor when she touch'd the keys,
Which told me she was there alone,
And uttering all her soul at ease.

I enter'd; for I did not choose
To learn how in her heart I throve,
By chance or stealth; beyond her use,
Her greeting flatter'd me with love.

2

With true love's treacherous confidence,
And ire, at last to laughter won,
She spoke this speech, and mark'd its sense,
By action, as her Aunt had done.

3

'"You, with your looks and catching air,
To think of Vaughan! You fool! You know,
You might, with ordinary care,
Ev'n yet be Lady Clitheroe.
You're sure he'll do great things some day!
Nonsense, he won't; he's dress'd too well.
Dines with the Sterling Club, they say;
Not commonly respectable!
Half Puritan, half Cavalier!
His curly hair I think's a wig;
And, for his fortune, why my Dear,
'Tis not enough to keep a gig.
Rich Aunts and Uncles never die;
And what you bring won't do for dress:
And so you'll live on By-and-by,
Within oaten-cake and water-cress!"

4

'I cried, but did not let her see.
At last she soften'd her dispraise,
On learning you had bought for me
A carriage and a pair of bays.
But here she comes! You take her in
To dinner. I impose this task
Make her approve my love; and win
What thanks from me you choose to ask!'

5

'My niece has told you every word
I said of you! What may I mean?
Of course she has; but you've not heard
How I abused you to the Dean; -
Yes, I'll take wine; he's mad, like her;
And she WILL have you: there it ends!
And, now I've done my duty, Sir,

And you've shown common-sense, we're friends!'

6

'Go, child, and see him out yourself,'
Aunt Maude said, after tea, 'and show
The place, upon that upper shelf,
Where Petrarch stands, lent long ago.'

7

'These rose-leaves to my heart be press'd,
Honoria, while it aches for you!'
(The rose in ruin, from her breast,
Fell, as I took a fond adieu.)
'You must go now, Love!' 'See, the air
Is thick with starlight!' 'Let me tie
This scarf on. Oh, your Petrarch! There!
I'm coming, Aunt!' 'Sweet, Sweet!' 'Good-bye!'
'Ah, Love, to me 'tis death to part,
Yet you, my sever'd life, smile on!'
These "Good-nights," Felix, break my heart;
I'm only gay till you are gone!'
With love's bright arrows from her eyes,
And balm on her permissive lips,
She pass'd, and night was a surprise,
As when the sun at Quito dips.
Her beauties were like sunlit snows,
Flush'd but not warm'd with my desire.
Oh, how I loved her! Fiercely glows
In the pure air of frost the fire.
Who for a year is sure of fate!
I thought, dishearten'd as I went,
Wroth with the Dean, who bade me wait,
And vex'd with her, who seem'd content.
Nay, could eternal life afford
That tyranny should thus deduct
From this fair land, which call'd me lord,
A year of the sweet usufruct?
It might not and it should not be!
I'd go back now, and he must own,
At once, my love's compulsive plea.
I turn'd, I found the Dean alone.
'Nonsense, my friend; go back to bed!
It's half-past twelve!' 'July, then, Sir!'
'Well, come to-morrow,' at last he said,
'And you may talk of it with her.'
A light gleam'd as I pass'd the stair.

A pausing foot, a flash of dress,
And a sweet voice. 'Is Felix there?'
'July, Love!' 'Says Papa so?' 'Yes!'

CANTO III.—THE COUNTRY BALL

PRELUDES

I.—LOVE CEREMONIOUS

Keep your undrest, familiar style
For strangers, but respect your friend,
Her most, whose matrimonial smile
Is and asks honour without end.
'Tis found, and needs it must so be,
That life from love's allegiance flags,
When love forgets his majesty
In sloth's unceremonious rags.
Let love make home a gracious Court;
There let the world's rude, hasty ways
Be fashion'd to a loftier port,
And learn to bow and stand at gaze;
And let the sweet respective sphere
Of personal worship there obtain
Circumference for moving clear,
None treading on another's train.
This makes that pleasures do not cloy,
And dignifies our mortal strife
With calmness and considerate joy,
Befitting our immortal life.

II.—THE RAINBOW.

A stately rainbow came and stood,
When I was young, in High-Hurst Park;
Its bright feet lit the hill and wood
Beyond, and cloud and sward were dark;
And I, who thought the splendour ours
Because the place was, t'wards it flew,
And there, amidst the glittering showers,
Gazed vainly for the glorious view.
With whatsoever's lovely, know
It is not ours; stand off to see,
Or beauty's apparition so
Puts on invisibility.

62

III.—A PARADOX.

To tryst Love blindfold goes, for fear
He should not see, and eyeless night
He chooses still for breathing near
Beauty, that lives but in the sight.

THE COUNTY BALL.

1

Well, Heaven be thank'd my first-love fail'd,
As, Heaven be thank'd, our first-loves do!
Thought I, when Fanny past me sail'd,
Loved once, for what I never knew,
Unless for colouring in her talk,
When cheeks and merry mouth would show
Three roses on a single stalk,
The middle wanting room to blow,
And forward ways, that charm'd the boy
Whose love-sick mind, misreading fate,
Scarce hoped that any Queen of Joy
Could ever stoop to be his mate.

2

But there danced she, who from the leaven
Of ill preserv'd my heart and wit
All unawares, for she was heaven,
Others at best but fit for it.
One of those lovely things she was
In whose least action there can be
Nothing so transient but it has
An air of immortality.
I mark'd her step, with peace elate,
Her brow more beautiful than morn,
Her sometime look of girlish state
Which sweetly waived its right to scorn;
The giddy crowd, she grave the while,
Although, as 'twere beyond her will,
Around her mouth the baby smile
That she was born with linger'd still.
Her ball-dress seem'd a breathing mist,
From the fair form exhaled and shed,
Raised in the dance with arm and wrist
All warmth and light, unbraceleted.
Her motion, feeling 'twas beloved,
The pensive soul of tune express'd,
And, oh, what perfume, as she moved,

Came from the flowers in her breast!
How sweet a tongue the music had!
'Beautiful Girl,' it seem'd to say,
'Though all the world were vile and sad,
Dance on; let innocence be gay.'
Ah, none but I discern'd her looks,
When in the throng she pass'd me by,
For love is like a ghost, and brooks
Only the chosen seer's eye;
And who but she could e'er divine
The halo and the happy trance,
When her bright arm reposed on mine,
In all the pauses of the dance!

3

Whilst so her beauty fed my sight,
And whilst I lived in what she said,
Accordant airs, like all delight
Most sweet when noted least, were play'd;
And was it like the Pharisee
If I in secret bow'd my face
With joyful thanks that I should be,
Not as were many, but with grace
And fortune of well-nurtured youth,
And days no sordid pains defile,
And thoughts accustom'd to the truth,
Made capable of her fair smile?

4

Charles Barton follow'd down the stair,
To talk with me about the Ball,
And carp at all the people there.
The Churchills chiefly stirr'd his gall:
'Such were the Kriemhilds and Isondes
You storm'd about at Trinity!
Nothing at heart but handsome Blondes!
'Folk say that you and Fanny Fry—'
'They err! Good-night! Here lies my course,
Through Wilton.' Silence blest my ears,
And, weak at heart with vague remorse,
A passing poignancy of tears
Attack'd mine eyes. By pale and park
I rode, and ever seem'd to see,
In the transparent starry dark,
That splendid brow of chastity,
That soft and yet subduing light,

At which, as at the sudden moon,
I held my breath, and thought 'how bright!'
That guileless beauty in its noon,
Compelling tribute of desires
Ardent as day when Sirius reigns,
Pure as the permeating fires
That smoulder in the opal's veins.

CANTO IV.—LOVE IN IDLENESS

PRELUDES.

I.—HONOUR AND DESERT.

O Queen, awake to thy renown,
Require what 'tis our wealth to give,
And comprehend and wear the crown
Of thy despised prerogative!
I, who in manhood's name at length
With glad songs come to abdicate
The gross regality of strength,
Must yet in this thy praise abate,
That, through thine erring humbleness
And disregard of thy degree,
Mainly, has man been so much less
Than fits his fellowship with thee.
High thoughts had shaped the foolish brow,
The coward had grasp'd the hero's sword,
The vilest had been great, hadst thou,
Just to thyself, been worth's reward.
But lofty honours undersold
Seller and buyer both disgrace;
And favours that make folly bold
Banish the light from virtue's face.

II.—LOVE AND HONOUR.

What man with baseness so content,
Or sick with false conceit of right,
As not to know that the element
And inmost warmth of love's delight
Is honour? Who'd not rather kiss
A duchess than a milkmaid, prank
The two in equal grace, which is
Precedent Nature's obvious rank?
Much rather, then, a woman deck'd

With saintly honours, chaste and good,
Whose thoughts celestial things affect,
Whose eyes express her heavenly mood!
Those lesser vaunts are dimm'd or lost
Which plume her name or paint her lip,
Extinct in the deep-glowing boast
Of her angelic fellowship.

III.—VALOUR MISDIRECTED.

I'll hunt for dangers North and South,
To prove my love, which sloth maligns!'
What seems to say her rosy mouth?
'I'm not convinced by proofs but signs.'

LOVE IN IDLENESS.

1

What should I do? In such a wife
Fortune had lavish'd all her store,
And nothing now seem'd left for life
But to deserve her more and more.
To this I vow'd my life's whole scope;
And Love said, 'I forewarn you now,
The Maiden will fulfill your hope
Only as you fulfil your vow.'

2

A promised service, (task for days),
Was done this morning while she slept,
With that full heart which thinks no praise
Of vows which are not more than kept;
But loftier work did love impose.
And studious hours. Alas, for these,
While she from all my thoughts arose
Like Venus from the restless seas!

3

I conn'd a scheme, within mind elate:
My Uncle's land would fall to me,
My skill was much in school debate,
My friends were strong in Salisbury;
A place in Parliament once gain'd,
Thro' saps first labour'd out of sight,
Far loftier peaks were then attain'd
With easy leaps from height to height;
And that o'erwhelming honour paid,

Or recognised, at least, in life,
Which this most sweet and noble Maid
Should yield to him who call'd her Wife.

4

I fix'd this rule: in Sarum Close
To make two visits every week,
The first, to-day; and, save on those,
I nought would do, think, read, or speak,
Which did not help my settled will
To earn the Statesman's proud applause.
And now, forthwith, to mend my skill
In ethics, politics, and laws,
The Statesman's learning! Flush'd with power
And pride of freshly-form'd resolve,
I read Helvetius half-an-hour;
But, halting in attempts to solve
Why, more than all things else that be,
A lady's grace hath force to move
That sensitive appetency
Of intellectual good, call'd love,
Took Blackstone down, only to draw
My swift-deriving thoughts ere long
To love, which is the source of law,
And, like a king, can do no wrong;
Then open'd Hyde, where loyal hearts,
With faith unpropp'd by precedent,
Began to play rebellious parts.
O, mighty stir that little meant!
How dull the crude, plough'd fields of fact
To me who trod the Elysian grove!
How idle all heroic act
By the least suffering of love!
I could not read; so took my pen,
And thus commenced, in form of notes,
A Lecture for the Salisbury men,
With due regard to Tory votes:
'A road's a road, though worn to ruts;
They speed who travel straight therein;
But he who tacks and tries short cuts
Gets fools' praise and a broken shin—'
And here I stopp'd in sheer despair;
But, what to-day was thus begun,
I vow'd, up starting from my chair,
To-morrow should indeed be done;
So loosed my chafing thoughts from school,

To play with fancy as they chose,
And then, according to my rule,
I dress'd, and came to Sarum Close.

5

Ah, that sweet laugh! Diviner sense
Did Nature, forming her, inspire
To omit the grosser elements,
And make her all of air and fire!

6

To-morrow, Cowes' Regatta fell:
The Dean would like his girls to go,
If I went too. 'Most gladly.' Well,
I did but break a foolish vow!
Unless Love's toil has love for prize,
(And then he's Hercules), above
All other contrarieties
Is labour contrary to love.
No fault of Love's, but nature's laws!
And Love, in idleness, lies quick;
For as the worm whose powers make pause,
And swoon, through alteration sick,
The soul, its wingless state dissolved,
Awaits its nuptial life complete,
All indolently self-convolved,
Cocoon'd in silken fancies sweet.

CANTO V.—THE QUEEN'S ROOM

PRELUDES.

I.—REJECTED.

'Perhaps she's dancing somewhere now!'
The thoughts of light and music wake
Sharp jealousies, that grow and grow
Till silence and the darkness ache.
He sees her step, so proud and gay,
Which, ere he spake, foretold despair:
Thus did she look, on such a day,
And such the fashion of her hair;
And thus she stood, when, kneeling low,
He took the bramble from her dress,
And thus she laugh'd and talk'd, whose 'No'
Was sweeter than another's 'Yes.'

He feeds on thoughts that most deject;
He impudently feigns her charms,
So reverenced in his own respect,
Dreadfully clasp'd by other arms;
And turns, and puts his brows, that ache,
Against the pillow where 'tis cold.
If, only now his heart would break!
But, oh, how much a heart can hold.

II.—RACHEL.

You loved her, and would lie all night
Thinking how beautiful she was,
And what to do for her delight.
Now both are bound with alien laws!
Be patient; put your heart to school;
Weep if you will, but not despair;
The trust that nought goes wrong by rule
Should ease this load the many bear.
Love, if there's heav'n, shall meet his dues,
Though here unmatch'd, or match'd amiss;
Meanwhile, the gentle cannot choose
But learn to love the lips they kiss.
Ne'er hurt the homely sister's ears
With Rachel's beauties; secret be
The lofty mind whose lonely tears
Protest against mortality.

III.—THE HEART'S PROPHECIES.

Be not amazed at life; 'tis still
The mode of God with his elect
Their hopes exactly to fulfil,
In times and ways they least expect.

THE QUEEN'S ROOM.

1

There's nothing happier than the days
In which young Love makes every thought
Pure as a bride's blush, when she says
'I will' unto she knows not what;
And lovers, on the love-lit globe,
For love's sweet sake, walk yet aloof,
And hear Time weave the marriage-robe,
Attraction warp and reverence woof.

69

2

My Housekeeper, my Nurse of yore,
Cried, as the latest carriage went,
'Well, Mr, Felix, Sir, I'm sure
The morning's gone off excellent!
I never saw the show to pass
The ladies, in their fine fresh gowns,
So sweetly dancing on the grass,
To music with its ups and downs.
We'd such work, Sir, to clean the plate;
'Twas just the busy times of old.
The Queen's Room, Sir, look'd quite like state.
Miss Smythe, when she went up, made bold
To peep into the Rose Boudoir,
And cried, "How charming! all quite new;"
And wonder'd who it could be for.
All but Miss Honor look'd in too.
But she's too proud to peep and pry.
None's like that sweet Miss Honor, Sir!
Excuse my humbleness, but I
Pray Heav'n you'll get a wife like her!
The Poor love dear Miss Honor's ways
Better than money. Mrs. Rouse,
Who ought to know a lady, says
No finer goes to Wilton House.
Miss Bagshaw thought that dreary room
Had kill'd old Mrs. Vaughan with fright;
She would not sleep in such a tomb
For all her host was worth a night!
Miss Fry, Sir, laugh'd; they talk'd the rest
In French; and French Sir's Greek to me;
But, though they smiled, and seem'd to jest,
No love was lost, for I could see
How serious-like Miss Honor was—'
'Well, Nurse, this is not my affair.
The ladies talk'd in French with cause.
Good-day; and thank you for your prayer.'

3

I loiter'd through the vacant house,
Soon to be her's; in one room stay'd,
Of old my mother's. Here my vows
Of endless thanks were oftenest paid.
This room its first condition kept;
For, on her road to Sarum Town,
Therein an English Queen had slept,

Before the Hurst was half pull'd down.
The pictured walls the place became:
Here ran the Brook Anaurus, where
Stout Jason bore the wrinkled dame
Whom serving changed to Juno; there,
Ixion's selfish hope, instead
Of the nuptial goddess, clasp'd a cloud;
And, here, translated Psyche fed
Her gaze on Love, not disallow'd.

4

And in this chamber had she been,
And into that she would not look,
My Joy, my Vanity, my Queen,
At whose dear name my pulses shook!
To others how express at all
My worship in that joyful shrine?
I scarcely can myself recall
What peace and ardour then were mine;
And how more sweet than aught below,
The daylight and its duties done,
It felt to fold the hands, and so
Relinquish all regards but one;
To see her features in the dark,
To lie and meditate once more
The grace I did not fully mark,
The tone I had not heard before;
And from my pillow then to take
Her notes, her picture, and her glove,
Put there for joy when I should wake,
And press them to the heart of love;
And then to whisper 'Wife!' and pray
To live so long as not to miss
That unimaginable day
Which farther seems the nearer 'tis;
And still from joy's unfathom'd well
To drink, in dreams, while on her brows
Of innocence ineffable
Blossom'd the laughing bridal rose.

CANTO VI.—THE LOVE LETTERS.

PRELUDES.

I.—LOVE'S PERVERSITY.

How strange a thing a lover seems
To animals that do not love!
Lo, where he walks and talks in dreams,
And flouts us with his Lady's glove;
How foreign is the garb he wears;
And how his great devotion mocks
Our poor propriety, and scares
The undevout with paradox!
His soul, through scorn of worldly care,
And great extremes of sweet and gall,
And musing much on all that's fair,
Grows witty and fantastical;
He sobs his joy and sings his grief,
And evermore finds such delight
In simply picturing his relief,
That 'plaining seems to cure his plight;
He makes his sorrow, when there's none;
His fancy blows both cold and hot;
Next to the wish that she'll be won,
His first hope is that she may not;
He sues, yet deprecates consent;
Would she be captured she must fly;
She looks too happy and content,
For whose least pleasure he would die;
Oh, cruelty, she cannot care
For one to whom she's always kind!
He says he's nought, but, oh, despair,
If he's not Jove to her fond mind!
He's jealous if she pets a dove,
She must be his with all her soul;
Yet 'tis a postulate in love
That part is greater than the whole;
And all his apprehension's stress,
When he's with her, regards her hair,
Her hand, a ribbon of her dress,
As if his life were only there;
Because she's constant, he will change,
And kindest glances coldly meet,
And, all the time he seems so strange,
His soul is fawning at her feet;

Of smiles and simple heaven grown tired,
He wickedly provokes her tears,
And when she weeps, as he desired,
Falls slain with ecstasies of fears;
He blames her, though she has no fault,
Except the folly to be his;
He worships her, the more to exalt
The profanation of a kiss;
Health's his disease, he's never well
But when his paleness shames her rose;
His faith's a rock-built citadel,
Its sign a flag that each way blows;
His o'erfed fancy frets and fumes;
And Love, in him, is fierce, like Hate,
And ruffles his ambrosial plumes
Against the bars of time and fate.

II.—THE POWER OF LOVE.

Samson the Mighty, Solomon
The Wise, and Holy David all
Must doff their crowns to Love, for none
But fell as Love would scorn to fall!
And what may fallen spirits win,
When stripes and precepts cannot move?
Only the sadness of all sin,
When look'd at in the light of Love.

THE LOVE-LETTERS.

1

'You ask, Will admiration halt,
Should spots appear within my Sun?
Oh, how I wish I knew your fault,
For Love's tired gaze to rest upon!
Your graces, which have made me great,
Will I so loftily admire,
Yourself yourself shall emulate,
And be yourself your own desire.
I'll nobly mirror you too fair,
And, when you're false to me your glass,
What's wanting you'll by that repair,
So bring yourself through me to pass.
O dearest, tell me how to prove
Goodwill which cannot be express'd;
The beneficial heart of love

73

Is labour in an idle breast.
Name in the world your chosen part,
And here I vow, with all the bent
And application of my heart
To give myself to your content.
Would you live on, home-worshipp'd, thus,
Not proudly high nor poorly low?
Indeed the lines are fall'n to us
In pleasant places! Be it so.
But would you others heav'nward move,
By sight not faith, while you they admire?
I'll help with zeal as I approve
That just and merciful desire.
High as the lonely moon to view
I'll lift your light; do you decree
Your place, I'll win it; for from you
Command inspires capacity.
Or, unseen, would you sway the world
More surely? Then in gracious rhyme
I'll raise your emblem, fair unfurl'd
With blessing in the breeze of time.
Faith removes mountains, much more love;
Let your contempt abolish me
If ought of your devisal prove
Too hard or high to do or be.'

2

I ended. 'From your Sweet-Heart, Sir,'
Said Nurse, 'The Dean's man brings it down.'
I could have kiss'd both him and her!
'Nurse, give him that, with half-a-crown.'
How beat my heart, how paused my breath,
When, with perversely fond delay,
I broke the seal, that bore a wreath
Of roses link'd with one of bay.

3

'I found your note. How very kind
To leave it there! I cannot tell
How pleased I was, or how you find
Words to express your thoughts so well.
The Girls are going to the Ball
At Wilton. If you can, DO come;
And any day this week you call
Papa and I shall be at home.
You said to Mary once—I hope

In jest—that women SHOULD be vain:
On Saturday your friend (her Pope),
The Bishop dined with us again.
She put the question, if they ought?
He turn'd it cleverly away
(For giddy Mildred cried, she thought
We MUST), with "What we must we may."
'Dear papa laugh'd, and said 'twas sad
To think how vain his girls would be,
Above all Mary, now she had
Episcopal authority.
But I was very dull, dear friend,
And went upstairs at last, and cried.
Be sure to come to-day, or send
A rose-leaf kiss'd on either side.
Adieu! I am not well. Last night
My dreams were wild: I often woke,
The summer-lightning was so bright;
And when it flash'd I thought you spoke.'

CANTO VII.—THE REVULSION.

PRELUDES

I.—JOY AND USE.

Can ought compared with wedlock be
For use? But He who made the heart
To use proportions joy. What He
Has join'd let no man put apart.
Sweet Order has its draught of bliss
Graced with the pearl of God's consent,
Ten times delightful in that 'tis
Considerate and innocent.
In vain Disorder grasps the cup;
The pleasure's not enjoy'd but spilt,
And, if he stoops to lick it up,
It only tastes of earth and guilt.
His sorry raptures rest destroys;
To live, like comets, they must roam;
On settled poles turn solid joys,
And sunlike pleasures shine at home.

II.—'SHE WAS MINE.'

'Thy tears o'erprize thy loss! Thy wife,

In what was she particular?
Others of comely face and life,
Others as chaste and warm there are,
And when they speak they seem to sing;
Beyond her sex she was not wise;
And there is no more common thing
Than kindness in a woman's eyes.
Then wherefore weep so long and fast,
Why so exceedingly repine!
Say, how has thy Beloved surpass'd
So much all others?' 'She was mine.'

THE REVULSION.

1

'Twas when the spousal time of May
Hangs all the hedge with bridal wreaths,
And air's so sweet the bosom gay
Give thanks for every breath it breathes,
When like to like is gladly moved,
And each thing joins in Spring's refrain,
'Let those love now who never loved;
Let those who have loved love again;'
That I, in whom the sweet time wrought,
Lay stretch'd within a lonely glade,
Abandon'd to delicious thought
Beneath the softly twinkling shade.
The leaves, all stirring, mimick'd well
A neighbouring rush of rivers cold,
And, as the sun or shadow fell,
So these were green and those were gold;
In dim recesses hyacinths droop'd,
And breadths of primrose lit the air,
Which, wandering through the woodland, stoop'd
And gather'd perfumes here and there;
Upon the spray the squirrel swung,
And careless songsters, six or seven.
Sang lofty songs the leaves among,
Fit for their only listener, Heaven.
I sigh'd, 'Immeasurable bliss
Gains nothing by becoming more!
Millions have meaning; after this
Cyphers forget the integer.'

2

And so I mused, till musing brought

76

A dream that shook my house of clay,
And, in my humbled heart, I thought,
To me there yet may come a day
With this the single vestige seen
Of comfort, earthly or divine,
My sorrow some time must have been
Her portion, had it not been mine.
Then I, who knew, from watching life,
That blows foreseen are slow to fall,
Rehearsed the losing of a wife,
And faced its terrors each and all.
The self-chastising fancy show'd
The coffin with its ghastly breath;
The innocent sweet face that owed
None of its innocence to death;
The lips that used to laugh; the knell
That bade the world beware of mirth;
The heartless and intolerable
Indignity of 'earth to earth;'
At morn remembering by degrees
That she I dream'd about was dead;
Love's still recurrent jubilees,
The days that she was born, won, wed;
The duties of my life the same,
Their meaning for the feelings gone;
Friendship impertinent, and fame
Disgusting; and, more harrowing none,
Small household troubles fall'n to me,
As, 'What time would I dine to-day?'
And, oh, how could I bear to see
The noisy children at their play.
Besides, where all things limp and halt,
Could I go straight, should I alone
Have kept my love without default,
Pitch'd at the true and heavenly tone?
The festal-day might come to mind
That miss'd the gift which more endears;
The hour which might have been more kind,
And now less fertile in vain tears;
The good of common intercourse,
For daintier pleasures, then despised,
Now with what passionate remorse,
What poignancy of hunger prized!
The little wrong, now greatly rued,
Which no repentance now could right;
And love, in disbelieving mood,

Deserting his celestial height.
Withal to know, God's love sent grief
To make me less the world's, and more
Meek-hearted: ah, the sick relief!
Why bow'd I not my heart before?

3

'What,' I exclaimed, with chill alarm,
'If this fantastic horror shows
The feature of an actual harm!'
And, coming straight to Sarum Close,
As one who dreams his wife is dead,
And cannot in his slumber weep,
And moans upon his wretched bed,
And wakes, and finds her there asleep,
And laughs and sighs, so I, not less
Relieved, beheld, with blissful start,
The light and happy loveliness
Which lay so heavy on my heart.

CANTO VIII.—THE KOH-I-NOOR.

PRELUDES

I.—IN LOVE.

If he's capricious she'll be so,
But, if his duties constant are,
She lets her loving favour glow
As steady as a tropic star;
Appears there nought for which to weep,
She'll weep for nought, for his dear sake;
She clasps her sister in her sleep;
Her love in dreams is most awake.
Her soul, that once with pleasure shook,
Did any eyes her beauty own,
Now wonders how they dare to look
On what belongs to him alone;
The indignity of taking gifts
Exhilarates her loving breast;
A rapture of submission lifts
Her life into celestial rest;
There's nothing left of what she was;
Back to the babe the woman dies,
And all the wisdom that she has
Is to love him for being wise.

She's confident because she fears;
And, though discreet when he's away,
If none but her dear despot hears,
She prattles like a child at play.
Perchance, when all her praise is said,
He tells the news, a battle won,
On either side ten thousand dead.
'Alas!' she says; but, if 'twere known,
She thinks, 'He's looking on my face!
I am his joy; whate'er I do,
He sees such time-contenting grace
In that, he'd have me always so!'
And, evermore, for either's sake,
To the sweet folly of the dove,
She joins the cunning of the snake,
To rivet and exalt his love;
Her mode of candour is deceit;
And what she thinks from what she'll say
(Although I'll never call her cheat),
Lies far as Scotland from Cathay.
Without his knowledge he was won;
Against his nature kept devout;
She'll never tell him how 'twas done,
And he will never find it out.
If, sudden, he suspects her wiles,
And hears her forging chain and trap,
And looks, she sits in simple smiles,
Her two hands lying in her lap.
Her secret (privilege of the Bard,
Whose fancy is of either sex),
Is mine; but let the darkness guard
Myst'ries that light would more perplex!

II.—LOVE THINKING.

What lifts her in my thought so far
Beyond all else? Let Love not err!
'Tis that which all right women are,
But which I'll know in none but her.
She is to me the only Ark
Of that high mystery which locks
The lips of joy, or speaks in dark
Enigmas and in paradox;
That potent charm, which none can fly,
Nor would, which makes me bond and free,
Nor can I tell if first 'twas I

79

Chose it, or it elected me;
Which, when I look intentest, lo,
Cheats most mine eyes, albeit my heart,
Content to feel and not to know,
Perceives it all in every part;
I kiss its cheek; its life divine
Exhales from its resplendent shroud;
Ixion's fate reversed is mine,
Authentic Juno seems a cloud;
I feel a blessed warmth, I see
A bright circumference of rays,
But darkness, where the sun should be,
Fills admiration with amaze;
And when, for joy's relief, I think
To fathom with the line of thought
The well from which I, blissful, drink,
The spring's so deep I come to nought.

III.—THE KISS.

'I saw you take his kiss!' ''Tis true.'
'O, modesty!' ''Twas strictly kept:
He thought me asleep; at least, I knew
He thought I thought he thought I slept.'

THE KOH-I-NOOR.

1

'Be man's hard virtues highly wrought,
But let my gentle Mistress be,
In every look, word, deed, and thought,
Nothing but sweet and womanly!
Her virtues please my virtuous mood,
But what at all times I admire
Is, not that she is wise or good,
But just the thing which I desire.
With versatility to sing
The theme of love to any strain,
If oft'nest she is anything,
Be it careless, talkative, and vain.
That seems in her supremest grace
Which, virtue or not, apprises me
That my familiar thoughts embrace
Unfathomable mystery.'

2

I answer'd thus; for she desired
To know what mind I most approved;
Partly to learn what she inquired,
Partly to get the praise she loved.

3

I praised her, but no praise could fill
The depths of her desire to please,
Though dull to others as a Will
To them that have no legacies.
The more I praised the more she shone,
Her eyes incredulously bright,
And all her happy beauty blown
Beneath the beams of my delight.
Sweet rivalry was thus begot;
By turns, my speech, in passion's style,
With flatteries the truth o'ershot,
And she surpass'd them with her smile.

4

'You have my heart so sweetly seiz'd,
And I confess, nay, 'tis my pride
That I'm with you so solely pleased,
That, if I'm pleased with aught beside,
As music, or the month of June,
My friend's devotion, or his wit,
A rose, a rainbow, or the moon,
It is that you illustrate it.
All these are parts, you are the whole;
You fit the taste for Paradise,
To which your charms draw up the soul
As turning spirals draw the eyes.
Nature to you was more than kind;
'Twas fond perversity to dress
So much simplicity of mind
In such a pomp of loveliness!
But, praising you, the fancy deft
Flies wide, and lets the quarry stray,
And, when all's said, there's something left,
And that's the thing I meant to say.'
'Dear Felix!' 'Sweet, my Love!' But there
Was Aunt Maude's noisy ring and knock!
'Stay, Felix; you have caught my hair.
Stoop! Thank you!' 'May I have that lock?'
'Not now. Good morning, Aunt!' 'Why, Puss,
You look magnificent to-day.'

'Here's Felix, Aunt.' 'Fox and green goose!
Who handsome gets should handsome pay!
Aunt, you are friends!' 'Ah, to be sure!
Good morning! Go on flattering, sir;
A woman, like the Koh-i-noor,
Mounts to the price that's put on her.'

CANTO IX.

PRELUDES.

I.—THE NURSLING OF CIVILITY.

Lo, how the woman once was woo'd;
Forth leapt the savage from his lair,
And fell'd her, and to nuptials rude
He dragg'd her, bleeding, by the hair.
From that to Chloe's dainty wiles
And Portia's dignified consent,
What distance! Bat these Pagan styles
How far below Time's fair intent!
Siegfried sued Kriemhild. Sweeter life
Could Love's self covet? Yet 'tis snug
In what rough sort he chid his wife
For want of curb upon her tongue!
Shall Love, where last I leave him, halt?
Nay; none can fancy or forsee
To how strange bliss may time exalt
This nursling of civility.

II.—THE FOREIGN LAND

A woman is a foreign land,
Of which, though there he settle young,
A man will ne'er quite understand
The customs, politics, and tongue.
The foolish hie them post-haste through,
See fashions odd, and prospects fair,
Learn of the language, 'How d'ye do,'
And go and brag they have been there.
The most for leave to trade apply,
For once, at Empire's seat, her heart,
Then get what knowledge ear and eye
Glean chancewise in the life-long mart.
And certain others, few and fit,
Attach them to the Court, and see

82

The Country's best, its accent hit,
And partly sound its polity.

III.—DISAPPOINTMENT

'The bliss which woman's charms bespeak,
I've sought in many, found in none!'
'In many 'tis in vain you seek
What only can be found in one.'

THE FRIENDS.

1

Frank's long, dull letter, lying by
The gay sash from Honoria's waist,
Reproach'd me; passion spared a sigh
For friendship without fault disgraced.
How should I greet him? how pretend
I felt the love he once inspired?
Time was when either, in his friend,
His own deserts with joy admired;
We took one side in school-debate,
Like hopes pursued with equal thirst,
Were even-bracketed by Fate,
Twin-Wranglers, seventh from the First;
And either loved a lady's laugh
More than all music; he and I
Were perfect in the pleasant half
Of universal charity.

2

From pride of likeness thus I loved
Him, and he me, till love begot
The lowliness which now approved
Nothing but that which I was not,
Blest was the pride of feeling so
Subjected to a girl's soft reign.
She was my vanity, and, oh,
All other vanities how vain!

3

Frank follow'd in his letter's track,
And set my guilty heart at ease
By echoing my excuses back
With just the same apologies.
So he had slighted me as well!
Nor was my mind disburthen'd less

When what I sought excuse to tell
He of himself did first confess.

4

Each, rapturous, praised his lady's worth;
He eloquently thus: 'Her face
Is the summ'd sweetness of the earth,
Her soul the glass of heaven's grace,
To which she leads me by the hand;
Or, briefly all the truth to say
To you, who briefly understand,
She is both heaven and the way.
Displeasures and resentments pass
Athwart her charitable eyes
More fleetingly than breath from glass,
Or truth from foolish memories;
Her heart's so touch'd with others' woes
She has no need of chastisement;
Her gentle life's conditions close,
Like God's commandments, with content,
And make an aspect calm and gay,
Where sweet affections come and go,
Till all who see her, smile and say,
How fair, and happy that she's so!
She is so lovely, true, and pure,
Her virtue virtue so endears,
That often, when I think of her,
Life's meanness fills mine eyes with tears—'
'You paint Miss Churchill! Pray go on—'
'She's perfect, and, if joy was much
To think her nature's paragon,
'Tis more that there's another such!'

5

Praising and paying back their praise
With rapturous hearts, t'ward Sarum Spire
We walk'd, in evening's golden haze,
Friendship from passion stealing fire.
In joy's crown danced the feather jest,
And, parting by the Deanery door,
Clasp'd hands, less shy than words, confess'd
We had not been true friends before.

CANTO X.

PRELUDES.

I.—FROST IN HARVEST

The lover who, across a gulf
Of ceremony, views his Love,
And dares not yet address herself,
Pays worship to her stolen glove.
The gulf o'erleapt, the lover wed,
It happens oft, (let truth be told),
The halo leaves the sacred head,
Respect grows lax, and worship cold,
And all love's May-day promising,
Like song of birds before they pair,
Or flush of flowers in boastful Spring,
Dies out, and leaves the Summer bare.
Yet should a man, it seems to me,
Honour what honourable is,
For some more honourable plea
Than only that it is not his.
The gentle wife, who decks his board
And makes his day to have no night,
Whose wishes wait upon her lord,
Who finds her own in his delight,
Is she another now than she
Who, mistress of her maiden charms,
At his wild prayer, incredibly
Committed them to his proud arms?
Unless her choice of him's a slur
Which makes her proper credit dim,
He never enough can honour her
Who past all speech has honour'd him.

II.—FELICITY

To marry her and take her home!
The poet, painting pureness, tells
Of lilies; figures power by Rome;
And each thing shows by something else.
But through the songs of poets look,
And who so lucky to have found
In universal nature's book
A likeness for a life so crown'd!
Here they speak best who best express

85

Their inability to speak,
And none are strong, but who confess
With happy skill that they are weak.

III.—MARRIAGE INDISSOLUBLE

'In heaven none marry.' Grant the most
Which may by this dark word be meant,
Who shall forbid the eternal boast
'I kiss'd, and kiss'd with her consent!'
If here, to Love, past favour is
A present boast, delight, and chain,
What lacks of honour, bond, and bliss,
Where Now and Then are no more twain!

THE EPITAPH.

1

'At Church, in twelve hours more, we meet!
This, Dearest, is our last farewell.'
'Oh, Felix, do you love me?' 'Sweet,
Why do you ask?' 'I cannot tell.'

2

And was it no vain fantasy
That raised me from the earth with pride?
Should I to-morrow verily
Be Bridegroom, and Honoria Bride?
Should I, in simple fact, henceforth
Live unconditionally lord
Of her whose smile for brightest worth
Seem'd all too bountiful reward?
Incredible life's promise seem'd,
Or, credible, for life too great;
Love his own deity blasphemed,
And doff'd at last his heavenly state.
What law, if man could mount so high,
To further insolence set bars,
And kept the chaste moon in the sky,
And bade him not tread out the stars!

3

Patience and hope had parted truce,
And, sun-like, Love obscured his ray
With dazzling mists, driven up profuse
Before his own triumphant way.
I thought with prayer how Jacob paid

86

The patient price of Rachel; them,
Of that calm grace Tobias said,
And Sarah's innocent 'Amen.'
Without avail! O'erwhelming wealth,
The wondrous gift of God so near,
Which should have been delight and health
Made heart and spirit sick and sere.
Until at last the soul of love,
That recks not of its own delight,
Awoke and bade the mists remove,
And then once more I breathed aright;
And I rehears'd my marriage vow,
And swore her welfare to prefer
To all things, and for aye as now
To live, not for myself, but her.
Forth, from the glittering spirit's peace
And gaiety ineffable,
Stream'd to the heart delight and ease,
As from an overflowing well;
And, orderly deriving thence
Its pleasure perfect and allow'd,
Bright with the spirit shone the sense,
As with the sun a fleecy cloud.
If now to part with her could make
Her pleasure greater, sorrow less,
I for my epitaph would take
'To serve seem'd more than to possess.'
And I perceiv'd, (the vision sweet
Dimming with happy dew mine eyes),
That love and joy are torches lit
From altar-fires of sacrifice.

4

Across the sky the daylight crept,
And birds grew garrulous in the grove,
And on my marriage-morn I slept
A soft sleep, undisturb'd by love.

CANTO XI.

PRELUDES.

I.—PLATONIC LOVE.

Right art thou who wouldst rather be
A doorkeeper in Love's fair house,

Than lead the wretched revelry
Where fools at swinish troughs carouse.
But do not boast of being least;
And if to kiss thy Mistress' skirt
Amaze thy brain, scorn not the Priest
Whom greater honours do not hurt.
Stand off and gaze, if more than this
Be more than thou canst understand,
Revering him whose power of bliss,
Angelic, dares to seize her hand,
Or whose seraphic love makes flight
To the apprehension of her lips;
And think, the sun of such delight
From thine own darkness takes eclipse.
And, wouldst thou to the same aspire,
This is the art thou must employ,
Live greatly; so shalt thou acquire
Unknown capacities of joy.

II.—A DEMONSTRATION.

Nature, with endless being rife,
Parts each thing into 'him' and 'her,'
And, in the arithmetic of life,
The smallest unit is a pair;
And thus, oh, strange, sweet half of me,
If I confess a loftier flame,
If more I love high Heaven than thee,
I more than love thee, thine I am;
And, if the world's not built of lies,
Nor all a cheat the Gospel tells,
If that which from the dead shall rise
Be I indeed, not something else,
There's no position more secure
In reason or in faith than this,
That those conditions must endure,
Which, wanting, I myself should miss.

III.—THE SYMBOL.

As if I chafed the sparks from glass,
And said, 'It lightens,' hitherto
The songs I've made of love may pass
For all but for proportion true;
But likeness and proportion both
Now fail, as if a child in glee,
Catching the flakes of the salt froth,

Cried, 'Look, my mother, here's the sea.
Yet, by the help of what's so weak,
But not diverse, to those who know,
And only unto those I speak,
May far-inferring fancy show
Love's living sea by coasts uncurb'd,
Its depth, its mystery, and its might,
Its indignation if disturb'd,
The glittering peace of its delight.

IV.—CONSTANCY REWARDED.

I vow'd unvarying faith, and she,
To whom in full I pay that vow,
Rewards me with variety
Which men who change can never know.

THE WEDDING.

1

Life smitten with a feverish chill,
The brain too tired to understand,
In apathy of heart and will,
I took the woman from the hand
Of him who stood for God, and heard
Of Christ, and of the Church his Bride;
The Feast, by presence of the Lord
And his first Wonder, beautified;
The mystic sense to Christian men;
The bonds in innocency made,
And gravely to be enter'd then,
For children, godliness, and, aid,
And honour'd, and kept free from smirch;
And how a man must love his wife
No less than Christ did love his Church,
If need be, giving her his life;
And, vowing then the mutual vow,
The tongue spoke, but intention slept.
'Tis well for us Heaven asks not how
We take this oath, but how 'tis kept.

2

O, bold seal of a bashful bound,
Which makes the marriage-day to be,
To those before it and beyond,
An iceberg in an Indian sea!

3

'Now, while she's changing,' said the Dean,
'Her bridal for her travelling dress,
I'll preach allegiance to your queen!
Preaching's the thing which I profess;
And one more minute's mine! You know
I've paid my girl a father's debt,
And this last charge is all I owe.
She's yours; but I love more than yet
You can; such fondness only wakes
When time has raised the heart above
The prejudice of youth, which makes
Beauty conditional to love.
Prepare to meet the weak alarms
Of novel nearness; recollect
The eye which magnified her charms
Is microscopic for defect.
Fear comes at first; but soon, rejoiced,
You'll find your strong and tender loves,
Like holy rocks by Druids poised,
The least force shakes, but none removes.
Her strength is your esteem; beware
Of finding fault; her will's unnerv'd
By blame; from you 'twould be despair;
But praise that is not quite deserv'd
Will all her noble nature move
To make your utmost wishes tree.
Yet think, while mending thus your Love,
Of snatching her ideal too.
The death of nuptial joy is sloth:
To keep your mistress in your wife,
Keep to the very height your oath,
And honour her with arduous life.
Lastly, no personal reverence doff.
Life's all externals unto those
Who pluck the blushing petals off,
To find the secret of the rose. -
How long she's tarrying! Green's Hotel
I'm sure you'll like. The charge is fair,
The wines good. I remember well
I stay'd once, with her Mother, there.
A tender conscience of her vow
That Mother had! She's so like her!'
But Mrs. Fife, much flurried, now
Whisper'd, 'Miss Honor's ready, Sir.'

4

Whirl'd off at last, for speech I sought,
To keep shy Love in countenance,
But, whilst I vainly tax'd my thought,
Her voice deliver'd mime from trance:
'Look, is not this a pretty shawl,
Aunt's parting gift.' 'She's always kind.'
'The new wing spoils Sir John's old Hall:
You'll see it, if you pull the blind.'

5

I drew the silk: in heaven the night
Was dawning; lovely Venus shone,
In languishment of tearful light,
Swathed by the red breath of the sun.

CANTO XII. HUSBAND AND WIFE

PRELUDES.

I.—THE MARRIED LOVER

Why, having won her, do I woo?
Because her spirit's vestal grace
Provokes me always to pursue,
But, spirit-like, eludes embrace;
Because her womanhood is such
That, as on court-days subjects kiss
The Queen's hand, yet so near a touch
Affirms no mean familiarness,
Nay, rather marks more fair the height
Which can with safety so neglect
To dread, as lower ladies might,
That grace could meet with disrespect,
Thus she with happy favour feeds
Allegiance from a love so high
That thence no false conceit proceeds
Of difference bridged, or state put by;
Because, although in act and word
As lowly as a wife can be,
Her manners, when they call me lord,
Remind me 'tis by courtesy;
Not with her least consent of will,
Which would my proud affection hurt,
But by the noble style that still

Imputes an unattain'd desert;
Because her gay and lofty brows,
When all is won which hope can ask,
Reflect a light of hopeless snows
That bright in virgin ether bask;
Because, though free of the outer court
I am, this Temple keeps its shrine
Sacred to Heaven; because, in short,
She's not and never can be mine.

II.—THE AMARANTH

Feasts satiate; stars distress with height;
Friendship means well, but misses reach,
And wearies in its best delight,
Vex'd with the vanities of speech;
Too long regarded, roses even
Afflict the mind with fond unrest;
And to converse direct within Heaven
Is oft a labour in the breast;
Whate'er the up-looking soul admires,
Whate'er the senses' banquet be,
Fatigues at last with vain desires,
Or sickens by satiety;
But truly my delight was more
In her to whom I'm bound for aye
Yesterday than the day before
And more to-day than yesterday.

HUSBAND AND WIFE.

1

I, while the shop-girl fitted on
The sand-shoes, look'd where, down the bay,
The sea glow'd with a shrouded sun.
'I'm ready, Felix; will you pay?'
That was my first expense for this
Sweet Stranger, now my three days' Wife.
How light the touches are that kiss
The music from the chords of life!

2

Her feet, by half-a-mile of sea,
In spotless sand left shapely prints;
With agates, then, she loaded me;
(The lapidary call'd them flints);

Then, at her wish, I hail'd a boat,
To take her to the ships-of-war,
At anchor, each a lazy mote
Black in the brilliance, miles from shore.

3

The morning breeze the canvas fill'd,
Lifting us o'er the bright-ridged gulf,
And every lurch my darling thrill'd
With light fear smiling at itself;
And, dashing past the Arrogant,
Asleep upon the restless wave
After its cruise in the Levant,
We reach'd the Wolf, and signal gave
For help to board; within caution meet,
My bride was placed within the chair,
The red flag wrapp'd about her feet,
And so swung laughing through the air.

4

'Look, Love,' she said, 'there's Frederick Graham,
My cousin, whom you met, you know,'
And seeing us, the brave man came,
And made his frank and courteous bow,
And gave my hand a sailor's shake,
And said, 'You ask'd me to the Hurst:
I never thought my luck would make
Your wife and you my guests the first.'
And Honor, cruel, 'Nor did we:
Have you not lately changed your ship?'
'Yes: I'm Commander, now,' said he,
With a slight quiver of the lip.
We saw the vessel, shown with pride;
Took luncheon; I must eat his salt!
Parting he said, (I fear my bride
Found him unselfish to a fault),
His wish, he saw, had come to pass,
(And so, indeed, her face express'd),
That that should be, whatever 'twas,
Which made his Cousin happiest.
We left him looking from above;
Rich bankrupt! for he could afford
To say most proudly that his love
Was virtue and its own reward.
But others loved as well as he,
(Thought I, half-anger'd), and if fate,

Unfair, had only fashion'd me
As hapless, I had been as great.

5

As souls, ambitious, but low-born,
If raised past hope by luck or wit,
All pride of place will proudly scorn,
And live as they'd been used to it,
So we two wore our strange estate:
Familiar, unaffected, free,
We talk'd, until the dusk grew late,
Of this and that; but, after tea,
As doubtful if a lot so sweet
As ours was ours in very sooth,
Like children, to promote conceit,
We feign'd that it was not the truth;
And she assumed the maiden coy,
And I adored remorseless charms,
And then we clapp'd our hands for joy,
And ran into each others arms.

THE EPILOGUE.

I

'Ah, dearest Wife, a fresh-lit fire
Sends forth to heaven great shows of fume,
And watchers, far away, admire;
But when the flames their power assume,
The more they burn the less they show,
The clouds no longer smirch the sky,
And then the flames intensest glow
When far-off watchers think they die.
The fumes of early love my verse
Has figured—' 'You must paint the flame!'
'Twould merit the Promethean curse!
But now, Sweet, for your praise and blame.'
'You speak too boldly; veils are due
To women's feelings.' 'Fear not this!
Women will vow I say not true,
And men believe thine lips they kiss.'
I did not call you "Dear" or "Love,"
'I think, till after Frank was born.'
'That fault I cannot well remove;
The rhymes'—but Frank now blew his horn,
And Walter bark'd, on hands and knees,

At Baby in the mignonette,
And all made, full-cry, for the trees
Where Felix and his Wife were set.
Again disturb'd, (crickets have cares!)
True to their annual use they rose,
To offer thanks at Evening Prayers
In three times sacred Sarum Close.

2

Passing, they left a gift of wine
At Widow Neale's. Her daughter said:
'O, Ma'am, she's sinking! For a sign,
She cried just now, of him that's dead,
"Mary, he's somewhere close above,
Weeping and wailing his dead wife,
With forceful prayers and fatal love
Conjuring me to come to life.
A spirit is terrible though dear!
It comes by night, and sucks my breath,
And draws me with desire and fear."
Ah, Ma'am, she'll soon be his in death!'

3

Vaughan, when his kind Wife's eyes were dry,
Said, 'This thought crosses me, my Dove;
If Heaven should proffer, when we die,
Some unconceiv'd, superior love,
How take the exchange without despair,
Without worse folly how refuse?'
But she, who, wise as she was fair,
For subtle doubts had simple clues,
Said, 'Custom sanctifies, and faith
Is more than joy: ah, how desire
In any heaven a different path,
Though, found at first, it had been higher?
Yet love makes death a dreadful thought!
Felix, at what a price we live!'
But present pleasures soon forgot
The future's dread alternative;
For, as became the festal time,
He cheer'd her heart with tender praise,
And speeches wanting only rhyme
To make them like his winged lays.
He discommended girlhood. 'What
For sweetness like the ten-years' wife,
Whose customary love is not

Her passion, or her play, but life?
With beauties so maturely fair,
Affecting, mild, and manifold,
May girlish charms mo more compare
Than apples green with apples gold.
Ah, still unpraised Honoria, Heaven,
When you into my arms it gave,
Left nought hereafter to be given
But grace to feel the good I have.'

4

Her own and manhood's modesty
Made dumb her love, but, on their road,
His hand in hers felt soft reply,
And like rejoinder found bestow'd;
And, when the carriage set them down,
'How strange,' said he, ''twould seem to meet,
When pacing, as we now this town,
A Florence or a Lisbon Street,
That Laura or that Catherine, who,
In the remote, romantic years,
From Petrarch or Camoens drew
Their songs and their immortal tears!'
But here their converse had its end;
For, crossing the Cathedral Lawn,
There came an ancient college-friend,
Who, introduced to Mrs. Vaughan,
Lifted his hat, and bow'd and smiled.
And fill'd her kind large eyes with joy,
By patting on the cheek her child,
With, 'Is he yours, this handsome boy?'

Printed in Great Britain
by Amazon